CIW Certification Prep

Study Guide for

1D0-541: CIW Database Design Specialist

Matthew Morris

Study Guide for CIW Database Design Specialist (Exam 1D0-541) Rev 1.0

ISBN-13: 978-1-941404-07-2
ISBN-10: 1941404073

Table of Contents

What to expect from the test

The test consists of 50 multiple choice questions and you have 90 minutes to complete it. The passing score listed on the CIW website at this time is 75%. Answer every question on the exam – an unanswered question counts off the same amount as an incorrect one. Take your time reading the question and all of the answers. You have almost two minutes per question and a significant number of questions are short. There is no reason to rush and potentially miss a question through haste.

This test is aimed at individuals just starting out a career with relational databases. This exam is intended to be completely vendor-neutral. Most of the information covered on the exam is relevant whether you plan to work with Oracle, MySQL or Microsoft SQL Server, or any other relational database. As a result of the target audience, the questions asked on 1D0-541 are at a fairly low level of difficulty – at least compared to the majority of certification exams that I have taken.

The information on this exam is largely about the concepts, theory and processes behind relational databases and developing applications based on relational databases. The developers of this test were almost certainly people that <u>teach</u> these concepts rather than actually <u>using</u> them to develop database applications. The test is big on textbook definitions and solutions. If you are new to the relational databases, that is likely not a problem. However, if (like me) you have been developing database applications for years, you may find that the correct answer is not what you would actually do in the real world.

Database developers should have a thorough understanding of how and why the relational model works. When preparing for this exam, take the time to really study the topics. If you find topics that are not clear to you, read another source on it to see if that helps your understanding. There are dozens of articles and websites that discuss relational theory, ERDs and requirements gathering. This is knowledge that you will use. It is worth spending the time to learn as much as possible.

What to Expect from this Study Guide

This book is built around the subject matter topics that CIW Certified has indicated will be tested. I have compiled and condensed material from numerous sources including database documentation, white papers, lectures and college course material published on the Web. It contains numerous diagrams and outputs from SQL operations that you are likely to see in exhibits during the test. The guide covers a significant percentage of the information that you must be familiar with in order to pass the exam.

What this guide is intended to do is to present the information that will be covered on the exam at the level it will likely be asked. The guide summarizes what each topic is about and presents details about it that you are likely to need for the exam. Because this is a study guide, it does not perform a deep dive into any single subject. You should use other sources in addition to this guide to gain a deeper insight into the material being tested. The ultimate goal of this guide is to present to you the concepts and information most likely to be the subject of test questions, and to do so in a very compact format that will allow you to read through it more than once to reinforce the information

That said, your ultimate goal – especially if you are new to database development – should be to learn as much about relational database concepts as possible. This is information that will be extremely useful if you plan to have a career as an Oracle developer or (to a somewhat lesser degree) as an Oracle database administrator. There are dozens of sites available on the Web that contain information about relational database concepts. Many university instructors have placed most (sometimes all) of their course curriculum online where it can be accessed freely. None of them will be an exact match for this exam. However, used in conjunction with this guide, they will provide the additional viewpoints and expansion to complement the material presented here.

Domain 1: Relational Database Fundamentals

1.1 Identify basic database types and management systems

What is a database?

A database in the broadest sense is anything that stores a collection of related information organized in a fashion that makes it easy to retrieve. By this definition, a box holding 3x5 index cards that contain recipes is a database. The cards contain information which is (probably) sorted and almost assuredly broken out by category (Meats, Cakes, Cookies, etc.) to make it easier to locate a given recipe. By the same token, a filing cabinet would also be considered a database. That said, no one ever called a recipe box or a filing cabinet a 'database' before the computer-based information storage systems of that name existed. Throughout the remainder of this guide, the term database will be in reference to a computer-based system for storing information.

A quick search of the Web brought up dozens of definitions for database, but they all have multiple elements in common. Four of the most typical definitions include:

- A database is a set of data that has a regular structure and that is organized in such a way that a computer can easily find the desired information.
- A comprehensive collection of related data organized for convenient access, generally in a computer.
- A database is a collection of information that is organized so that it can easily be accessed, managed, and updated.
- A database is information organized in such a way that a computer program can quickly select pieces of data.

All of these (plus my original definition) indicate that the information must be organized. It is imperative for a database to have some logic to the way in which the data gets stored. In the recipe card example, if the container for the 3x5 index cards was in fact a 2-foot by 2-foot cardboard box and the cards were simply tossed in at random, the result would not be a database. In addition to organization, each of the definitions refers to retrieving the data easily. In large part, this is why the data must be organized. However, just because data is organized does not guarantee that it can be retrieved easily. Imagine the recipes in our box are sorted from lowest to highest calorie count per serving. The data is organized, but that organization will not make it simple to find any given recipe. If there is no provision for locating the stored information, it is not really a database.

Organizations generate data constantly simply by the actions they take as part of their business processes. Many different events will generate data for a given company:

- When something is bought.
- When something is sold.
- When they gain a new customer.
- When they bid for a contract.
- When employees are paid.

Prior to computer-based databases, all of this information was paper-based. The resulting papers were generally stored in filing cabinets and only a tiny fraction of the paperwork was ever used outside of audits and fact-checking. Since PCs are now a given, the information is more often stored in text files, spreadsheets and word processor documents.

While these files are now stored on a computer rather than a file cabinet, the problems of retrieving the information still exist. If this organization has 1,000 employees, each with their own computer holding dozens of such files, it becomes difficult to locate any one piece of data. In addition, depending on the job role of the employee in question, critical data about the company's finances, or private data about employees would be on various computers in the offices stored as simple files. The growing usage of databases -- particularly relational databases has allowed companies to start putting their data into a form that allows them to organize, protect, and retrieve information from. This includes information such as:

- How many items of this type has the company bought in the past?
- What are the sales for the past three quarters? Are sales for this item increasing or decreasing year over year?
- Where are the majority of their customers located?
- What is the percentage of contracts bid for vs. contracts won?
- How do the salaries paid by the organization stack up to industry standards?

All of the above questions can be answered using a paper-based system and a lot of legwork. However, if the data has been stored in a relational database, the answers can be obtained much more rapidly and cheaply. When it costs time and money to obtain information, companies often make decisions in the absence of information -- sometimes with disastrous results.

A computer-based database system is more than just a set of files stored on a hard drive. The complete system includes the users of the database and all of the elements between. A database management system provides a method to centralize the storage of information, organize it, and provide vastly improved control. It allows users to create, edit and update information in database files. Once information has been entered into the database, it is possible easily retrieve data as needed. Specifically, a DBMS provides the following capabilities:

- **Concurrency** -- Simultaneous access to a database by multiple users.
- **Integrity** -- A well-designed database contains rules that ensure the integrity of the data.
- **Security** -- Access to data elements can be restricted depending on their job role.
- **Safety** -- A database administrator is generally responsible for backing-up the data regularly so that it can be recovered in the event of a failure.

A well-designed database application should also reduce duplication of data entry. Often the same information will be required by multiple people within an organization. In a non-DBMS model, each of these people might well enter this information into 'their' spreadsheet. In a DBMS-based environment, only a single copy of any given piece of information should be entered and it will be accessible by anyone whose job role requires it. The four parts of a database system are:

- **Database** -- The database itself is information stored on disk in one or more operating system files. For a relational database (the main focus of this exam), the files will contain information about tables, indexes, and other structures that comprise the logical database elements.
- **Database Management System (DBMS)** -- The DBMS is the software program that is used to administer the database. It is in complete control of the contents of the database files. It accepts commands via SQL and processes those commands to add, update, delete, or retrieve data from the database.
- **Database Application** -- This is the application that acts as an intermediary between the DBMS and the users. The database application can be one in which users send SQL directly to the RDBMS (Oracle's SQL*Plus would be an example). Alternately the database application may provide an interface where users have little or no direct SQL communication with the database, instead using forms to enter and retrieve data. PeopleSoft is an application commonly used by human resources departments where users may never use SQL directly to interface with the RDBMS.
- **Users** -- Users are the final element of a database system. They enter, update, delete, and retrieve information from the database through one or more database applications. They may issue SQL directly or make use of forms and reports provided by a database application.

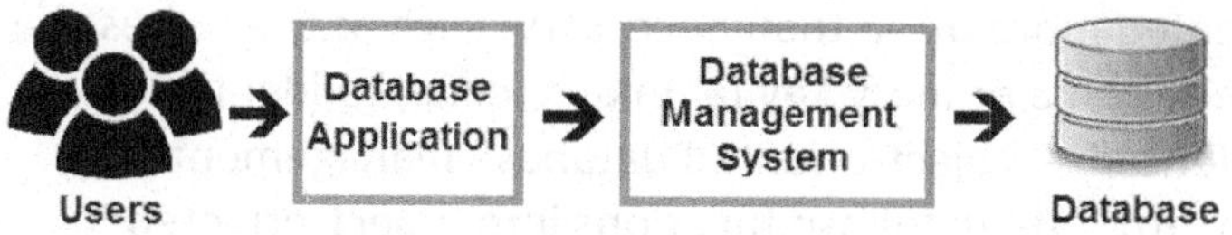

Types of database models

Once computers began to have the storage capacity and computing power required to hold and process significant quantities of information, the first Database Management Systems (DBMS) were developed. A DBMS facilitates the operations required to store, organize, and retrieve information in a database. There are several different models around which a database management system can be designed. The specific model used dictates how information is organized in the files used by the management system. The data organization has implications on the flexibility and performance of the database application. Some of the most common database models include:

- **Flat** -- Flat file databases are the simplest model there is. They have very little flexibility, consisting of only two dimensions (rows and columns). They cannot contain complex data relationships. However, they are still commonly used as a means for transferring data between systems. Delimited or fixed-width text files are effectively flat-file databases and almost every DBMS has the ability to read and import data from them.
- **Hierarchical** -- In this model, the data is organized into a tree-like structure. Information can be represented using parent/child relationships: each parent can have many children, but each child has only one parent. This is also known as a one-to-many relationship.
- **Network** -- As with the hierarchical database model, the network model structures data as a tree of records. However, while the hierarchical model allows each child only one parent, the network model allows each record to have multiple parent and child records, forming a generalized graph structure
- **Relational** -- The relational model is based on first-order predicate logic. In the relational model, all data is represented in terms of tuples, grouped into relations. Tables are normalized so that data

is not repeated more often than necessary. Each of the tuples in a table depends on a primary key (a unique value) to identify it.

- **Object Oriented** -- Object-oriented database management systems incorporate database functions into object-oriented programming languages. OODBMSs allow developers working within an object-oriented language to store data in the form of objects, and then replicate or modify existing objects to make new objects within the database. The database is closely integrated with the programming language, allowing the programmer to maintain consistency within a single environment.

The evolution of databases

Flat file databases are is the least complex form of storage system and were the first to be broadly utilized. Flat files have been used as a means of storing data for decades. The nature of flat files makes them unsuitable for large databases. However, their very simplicity means that they are unlikely to ever disappear completely. They are still commonly used to store configuration data for software packages and operating system parameter files. Some of the advantages and disadvantages of flat file databases include:

Advantages

- The files are generally very easy to understand.
- They are the easiest database to implement (for small amounts of data at least).
- There is no proprietary software required to implement them.
- The records are all stored in a single location.
- Flat files are completely platform independent.

Disadvantages

- Flat files have very little security. Unless the file is encrypted (which negates many of its advantages) it is easy to extract information.

- There is no DBMS or rules to enforce data consistency.
- Redundant data is common in flat files.
- When the files are very large, accessing and updating data can be slow. A single change can require rewriting the entire file.
- Searching for specific data can be time consuming due to a lack of indexing.

Flat file databases generally require that information about each different type of entity be stored in separate files. Throughout this guide I will use elements of a hypothetical database for a small airline company called 'Imaginary Airlines'. In this example, Imaginary Airlines needs to store information about a set of airports they serve, a set of aircraft types that they own one or more of, and where each of their fleet of aircraft are based, conceivably they might use a set of three comma-delimited files like the following:

```
AIRPORTS.CSV
-------------------------------------------
'Orlando, FL','MCO'
'Atlanta, GA','ATL'
'Miami, FL','MIA'
'Jacksonville, FL','JAX'
'Dallas/Fort Worth','DFW'
'Houston, TX','IAH'
'New York, NY - Kennedy','JFK'
'Los Angeles, CA','LAX'

AIRCRAFT_TYPES.CSV
-------------------------------------------
'Boeing 747', 'Wide', 'Double', 416
'Boeing 767', 'Wide', 'Single', 350
'Boeing 737', 'Narrow', 'Single', 200
'Boeing 757', 'Narrow', 'Single', 240
'Boeing 777', 'Wide', 'Single', 407
'Boeing 787', 'Wide', 'Single', 296
'Airbus A320', 'Narrow', 'Single', 200
'Airbus A380', 'Wide', 'Double', 525

AIRCRAFT_FLEET.CSV
-------------------------------------------
'Dallas/Fort Worth','DFW','Boeing 747'
'Miami, FL','MIA','Boeing 747'
'Miami, FL','MIA','Boeing 747'
'Dallas/Fort Worth','DFW','Boeing 767'
'Orlando, FL','MCO','Boeing 767'
'Orlando, FL','MCO','Boeing 767'
'Atlanta, GA','ATL','Boeing 737'
'Atlanta, GA','ATL','Boeing 757'
```

The third file in particular shows one of the failings of flat files. The airports and aircraft types get repeated multiple times. This is redundant data and can cause problems with data consistency in large databases.

A variant of a flat file database is a file based system. This is a collection of individual applications that allow users to access information in the files. Each application in a file based system defines and manages its data separately from the others.

Advantages

- They are a better alternative to paper based filing systems.

Disadvantages

- Data among different applications is separated and isolated.
- Data is dependent on multiple applications.
- There is significant data duplication.
- Data between applications is incompatible.
- There is a lack of flexibility in organizing and querying the data.
- Requires multiple different application programs.

Following on the heels of flat file databases, the Hierarchical Data Model was the earliest true Database Management System to see widespread use. One of the first hierarchical databases was the Information Management System (IMF) created by IBM. IMF was a precursor to relational database management systems. The hierarchical model is a method for organizing a database that uses multiple one to many relationships. In this model, the guiding principle is that one parent can have many children but children are allowed only a single parent. It is common for information in the real world to map well under a one-to-many relationship.

Advantages:

- It allows easy addition and deletion of new information.
- Data at the top of the Hierarchy is very fast to access.
- It relates very well to natural hierarchies such employee organization in corporations.
- It relates well to anything that works through a one to many relationship.

Disadvantages:

- It does not work well with sophisticated relationships.
- Data is often repetitively stored in many different entities.
- Searching for information on the lower entities can be very slow.
- Searches must run through the entire model from top to bottom until the required information is found.
- Many to many relationships are not supported.

Using Imaginary Airlines as an example again, the below diagram shows how data for various tables might be related using a hierarchical database. It is worth noting that the three tables used in the flat file model example would not work well in the hierarchical model. The 'AIRCRAFT FLEET' data has two parents: 'AIRPORTS' and 'AIRCRAFT TYPES'. The hierarchical database model, unlike flat files, is no longer widely used.

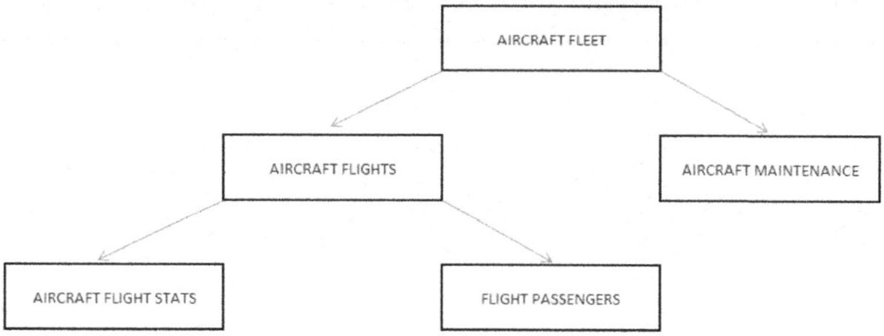

The Network model was developed largely as a means of resolving the biggest limitation of the hierarchical model. Where the hierarchical database model structures data with each record having a single parent record and many children, the network model allows a given record to have multiple child record and multiple parent records. The network model allows for a much more flexible organization of relationships between entities when compared to the hierarchic model. The model was widely implemented but was eventually displaced by the relational model. There are a few advantages and disadvantages of using the network database model.

Advantages

- Conceptually, the model is simpler than the relational model
- It allows for more data access flexibility than the hierarchical model.
- It can handle more relationship types than the hierarchical model.

Disadvantages

- The data structure is difficult to change.
- The relationships in large databases can become very complex.
- The model lacks structural independence.

The diagram below extends on the previous one for the hierarchical model. It demonstrates how the network model can account for the multi-parent nature of the 'AIRCRAFT FLEET' entity.

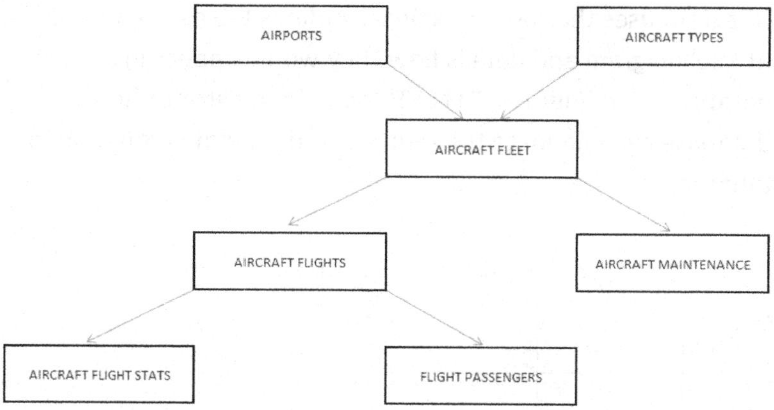

The relational model came on the scene after the preceding three and has proved flexible enough to supplant them and to continue to dominate even after the development of the object-oriented database model. In the relational model, entities (tables) contain key fields which are used to link together related records. The relational model provides a declarative method for specifying data to be stored. Entities in a relational database can have one to one, one to many, and many to many relationships.

Advantages

- Changes in the database structure do not affect data access, providing structural independence.
- The database design, maintenance, administration and usage is easier than the other models.
- SQL allows for ad hoc query capability.

Disadvantages

- Relational databases require more processing power than a comparably sized database under the other models.
- The ease of use makes it simpler to create poorly designed databases.

The below diagram uses the three Imaginary Airlines tables from the original 'Flat File' diagram and details how they would appear in a relational database. The 'AIRCRAFT FLEET' table demonstrates how a relational database can eliminate the redundant data that is common in flat file databases.

AIRPORTS

APT_ID	APT_NAME	APT_ABBR
1	Orlando, FL	MCO
2	Atlanta, GA	ATL
3	Miami, FL	MIA
4	Jacksonville, FL	JAX
5	Dallas/Fort Worth	DFW
7	Houston, TX	IAH

AIRCRAFT FLEET

AFL_ID	ACT_ID	APT_ID
1	2	1
2	2	1
3	3	2
4	4	2
5	1	3
6	1	3
7	1	5
8	2	5

AIRCRAFT TYPES

ACT_ID	ACT_NAME	ACT_BODY	ACT_DECKS	ACT_SEATS
1	Boeing 747	Wide	Double	416
2	Boeing 767	Wide	Single	350
3	Boeing 737	Narrow	Single	200
4	Boeing 757	Narrow	Single	240
5	Boeing 777	Wide	Single	407
6	Boeing 787	Wide	Single	296

Origins of relational databases

E. F. Codd defined a relational model based on mathematical set theory in 1970. Databases designed around the relational model are the most widely used today. Prior to the relational model, data was stored in rigid relationships that could not be modified easily using a Data Definition Language (DDL). The relational model provides a structure for a logical view of the data to be stored. It uses a number of mathematical constructs for this: domains, relations, tuples, and attributes. Each of these constructs have names that are used in databases. Domains for example define the data type being stored (i.e. character, number, date). In addition to the data structure, the relational model defines how data will be manipulated using relational algebra. It also defines the means for specifying and enforcing data integrity.

Codd's paper was essentially a mathematical exercise and used several terms that really only matter when you are performing relational algebra. In nineteen years working with RDBMS's, I have never found a need to use relational algebra. However, you will need to understand the premise of relational algebra as well as knowing the meaning of some of the terms used in relational theory for the exam. Relational algebra will be discussed in greater detail in a later section of this guide.

Codd's 12 Rules:

E.F. Codd produced a group of rules known as Codd's twelve rules. This is actually a set of thirteen rules that are numbered zero through twelve. The rules are intended to define the requirements that must be met by a DBMS in order for it to be considered a relational database management system (RDBMS). The full thirteen rules are very stringent and are not followed by any widely used RDBMS in existence. A handful of academic RDBMS systems strive to comply with the full set of rules.

- **Rule 0: The Foundation rule** -- For any system that is advertised as, or claimed to be, a relational data base management system, that system must be able to manage data bases entirely through its relational capabilities.
- **Rule 1: The information rule** -- All information in a relational data base is represented explicitly at the logical level and in exactly one way — by values in tables.
- **Rule 2: The guaranteed access rule** -- Each and every datum (atomic value) in a relational data base is guaranteed to be logically accessible by resorting to a combination of table name, primary key value and column name.
- **Rule 3: Systematic treatment of null values** -- Null values (distinct from the empty character string or a string of blank characters and distinct from zero or any other number) are supported in fully relational DBMS for representing missing information and inapplicable information in a systematic way, independent of data type.
- **Rule 4: Dynamic online catalog based on the relational model** -- The data base description is represented at the logical level in the same way as ordinary data, so that authorized users can apply the

same relational language to its interrogation as they apply to the regular data.

- **Rule 5: The comprehensive data sublanguage rule** -- A relational system may support several languages and various modes of terminal use (for example, the fill-in-the-blanks mode). However, there must be at least one language whose statements are expressible, per some well-defined syntax, as character strings and that is comprehensive in supporting all of the following items:
    - Data definition.
    - View definition.
    - Data manipulation (interactive and by program).
    - Integrity constraints.
    - Authorization.
    - Transaction boundaries (begin, commit and rollback).
- **Rule 6: The view updating rule** -- All views that are theoretically updatable are also updatable by the system.
- **Rule 7: High-level insert, update, and delete** -- The capability of handling a base relation or a derived relation as a single operand applies not only to the retrieval of data but also to the insertion, update and deletion of data.
- **Rule 8: Physical data independence** -- Application programs and terminal activities remain logically unimpaired whenever any changes are made in either storage representations or access methods.
- **Rule 9: Logical data independence** -- Application programs and terminal activities remain logically unimpaired when information-preserving changes of any kind that theoretically permit unimpairment are made to the base tables.
- **Rule 10: Integrity independence** -- Integrity constraints specific to a particular relational data base must be definable in the relational data sublanguage and storable in the catalog, not in the application programs.
- **Rule 11: Distribution independence** -- A relational DBMS has distribution independence.
- **Rule 12: The non-subversion rule** -- If a relational system has a low-level (single-record-at-a-time) language, that low level cannot be used to subvert or bypass the integrity rules and constraints expressed in the higher level relational language (multiple-records-at-a-time).

Relational databases and Database Management Systems (DBMSs)

A Database Management System (DBMS) performs a number of functions to ensure data integrity and consistency of data in the database. These functions include:

- A user-accessible catalog
- Transaction support
- Concurrency control
- Backup and recovery
- Authorization
- Data integrity
- Data independence
- Data communication

Today, Relational Database Management Systems (RDBMS) dominate the market of databases used by enterprise organizations. The flexibility and power inherent to the RDBMS make them ideal for the storage and quick retrieval of the data that organizations need in order to remain competitive.

Tables are the primary logical element in a relational database. In fact, the term 'relation' in relational algebra refers to what is commonly considered a table. Specifically a relation is a set of tuples (rows). The name "relational model" comes from the fact that relations (tables) are the central object. A table is a 2-dimensional structure that consists of closely related columns and zero or more rows. Some rules that tables must follow include:

- Each column must have a distinct name.
- All values in a column must conform to the same data format.
- Each row/column intersection represents a single data value.
- Row and column orders are inconsequential.
- Each table must have a primary key.
- The primary key is an attribute (or a combination of attributes) that uniquely identifies each row.

The diagram below shows a typical (albeit simple) table in a relational database. The table has three columns (attributes), one of which is the primary key. Three rows (tuples) of the table are displayed. The potential number of rows is limited only by available space.

Table (relation) name → **AIRPORTS**
Primary key attribute → PK
Column (attribute) name → APT_ID
Rows (tuples) →

APT_ID	APT_NAME	APT_ABBR
1	Orlando, FL	MCO
2	Atlanta, GA	ATL
3	Miami, FL	MIA

The physical data stored in an RDBMS is independent from the logical data structures designed to represent it. Logical data structures are stored in a database schema. A schema is a collection of logical data structures which are also referred to as schema objects. In the Oracle database, each schema is owned by and has the same name as a database user. Schema objects refer to the data in the database and are created by the user via Data Definition Language. Two of the more important schema objects are tables and indexes:

- **Table** -- Used to store the information, tables are defined with a name and a one or more columns. Each column in a table has a name and data type. Columns may also be defined with a maximum size and rules (known as integrity constraints) that determine whether or not data can be entered into them.
- **Index** -- Can optionally be created against one or more columns of a table. Indexes can be used to speed up access when querying a table. Unique indexes can also be used to ensure that no duplicate data is entered into a table.

1.2 List common database languages and their purposes, and identify language subsets of Structured Query Language (SQL).

Database languages

There a number of different languages that developers use routinely to interact with relational databases. The 500-pound gorilla is certainly the SQL language. While I'll list several other languages in this section, developers who use any of the others in developing database applications will also utilize SQL as well.

- **SQL** -- SQL is the primary means for communicating with a relational database. It is a nonprocedural language that allows users to specify a desired result rather than the actions required to achieve that result. Using SQL, a user can issue a command to select all rows from a given table and the RDBMS will determine the exact steps required in order to retrieve and display the results.
- **PL/SQL** – PL/SQL (Procedural Language / SQL) is Oracle's proprietary language that adds procedural aspects. It is tightly integrated with the SQL engine enabling developers to use all of the Oracle Database SQL statements, functions, and data types and allows developers to extend the capabilities of SQL with various capabilities associated with procedural languages including loops, if-then constructs, storing and retrieving data from variables, branching operations, and so on.
- **T-SQL** -- T-SQL (Transact-SQL) is comparable to PL/SQL, but it is proprietary to Sybase and Microsoft SQL Server. It provides a set of programming extensions that includes procedural programming, local variables, transaction control, exception and error handling, row processing, and declared variables.
- **Java** -- Java was expressly designed for use in the distributed environment of the Internet. However, Oracle incorporated a Java Virtual machine into their database. This allows Java applications to be used to create applications directly inside the database. Java applications inside the Oracle database have access to a data-processing engine that supports complex queries and different views of the same data. As with PL/SQL, this provides a robust

procedural environment in which to make applications to work with the database.

Introduction to Structured Query Language

Structured Query Language, almost always referred to as SQL (pronounced either see-kwell or as separate letters: ess-kyu-ell), is a programming language that was designed for managing items held in databases. SQL was originally based upon relational algebra and tuple relational calculus. Despite not entirely adhering to the relational model as described by Codd, SQL has become the most widely used database language in existence.

SQL statements enable you to perform the following tasks:

- Query the database
- Insert, update, and delete rows in a table
- Create, replace, alter, and drop objects
- Control access to the database and its objects
- Guarantee database consistency and integrity

Although there are dialects of SQL for different database vendors, it is nevertheless the closest thing to a standard query language that currently exists. In 1986, ANSI approved a rudimentary version of SQL as the official standard. However, most vendors have included many extensions to the ANSI standard in their products. Many vendors support mostly ANSI-compliant SQL, but few (if any) are 100% compliant.

The SQL language is used by many databases to access and store data. It allows users to not only query and modify data, but also to communicate with the DBMS to add new tables or other database objects, control numerous database settings, and perform maintenance operations. While many GUIs exist that allow users to interact graphically with relational database -- at their base, the interfaces are using SQL to power this interaction.

Any multi user database must be able to manage data access and updates from several sources simultaneously without corrupting data or providing erroneous information to users. Three concepts are critical to multi-user databases:

- **Transaction Management** -- When an operation against the database is broken into several steps, it is often necessary to ensure that all of the steps succeed or none of them. A transaction is a logical, atomic unit of work that contains one or more SQL statements. When any of the SQL statements fails to complete, transaction management guarantees that any statements in the transaction which have already been executed will have their changes rolled back.
- **Data Concurrency** -- This is defined as simultaneous access of the same data by multiple users. If no concurrency controls exist, it would be possible for users to cause changes that would compromise data integrity. When one user is modifying data in a table, other users must be prevented from modifying the same data (or the underlying structure of the table) until the first user's transaction has been completed. Relational databases use locks to control concurrent data access. Locks prevent destructive interactions between transactions while allowing concurrent access to data wherever possible.
- **Data Consistency** -- When multiple users are changing and querying data simultaneously, it is important that the data visible to database users is always consistent. If one user runs a transaction giving all employees a five percent raise while another user queries employee salaries, the query should not return data where some people have the raise and some do not. The DBMS enforces statement-level read consistency. The data returned by a query will always be consistent for a single point in time. Users can see their own uncommitted data in queries, but will never see uncommitted transactions initiated by other users.

The SQL language is split into four broad categories:

- **Data Definition Language (DDL)** -- DDL statements define, structurally change, and drop schema objects in the database.
- **Data Control Language (DCL)** – DCL statements are used to control access to data stored in a database.
- **Data Manipulation Language (DML)** -- DML statements query or manipulate data in existing schema objects. DML statements do not change the structure of the database, the only query or change the contents of the database.
- **Transaction Control Language (TCL)** – Transaction control statements are used to begin and end transactions. Transactions can be ended by reversing the changes just made or by making them permanent.

Data definition language

The data dictionary of a relational database is a set or tables that contain the information about all of the user objects in the database (tables, indexes, users, views, etc.) Data Definition Language (DDL) statements are used to make changes to the data dictionary. They are utilized to perform the following tasks (among others):

- Create, alter, and drop schema objects
- Analyze information on a table, index, or cluster

Some examples of the types of objects that are acted on by DDL commands include:

- **TABLE** -- The basic structure to hold user data.
- **INDEX** -- A schema object that contains an entry for each value that appears in one or more columns of a table and provides direct, fast access to rows.
- **VIEW** -- A logical table based on one or more tables or views, although it contains no data itself.
- **CONSTRAINT** -- A rule that restricts the values in a database column.

- **USER** -- An account through which database users can log in to the database and which provides the basis for creating schema objects.

Taking users as an example database object class, there are three basic DDL commands that will operate on it:

- **CREATE USER** – Creates a new user account in the relational database.
- **ALTER USER** – Makes a change to an existing user account.
- **DROP USER** – Removes an existing user account from the database.

The same three commands (CREATE, ALTER, DROP) exist for most objects in a database. DDL will be explored in greater detail in Domain 4.2.

Data manipulation language

Data Manipulation Language (DML) is the name given to the SQL statements used to manage data in a relational database. DML statements include INSERT, UPDATE, DELETE and MERGE. Each of these statements manipulates data in tables.

The SELECT statement is often grouped with the other four commands under the DML class of SQL operations. However, SELECT statements do not add, alter, or remove rows from database tables – so no data manipulation is involved. However, if the SELECT command is not included with DML, then it has no place to be. It certainly does not fit in with Data Definition Language (DDL), Data Control Language (DCL), or Transaction Control Language (TCL). Just be aware that when reference is made to DML statements, the context may include SELECT operations, but as a general rule will not.

Data manipulation language statements are utilized to manage data in existing schema objects. DML statements do not modify information in the data dictionary and do not implicitly commit the current transaction. The most commonly identified DML commands are:

- **INSERT** – Used to populate data in tables. It is possible to insert one row into one table, one row into multiple tables, multiple rows into one table, or multiple rows into multiple tables.
- **UPDATE** – Used to alter data that has already been inserted into a database table. An UPDATE can affect a single row or multiple rows, and a single column or multiple columns. The WHERE clause will determine which rows in the table are altered. When executed with no WHERE clause, it will update all rows in the target table. A single UPDATE statement can only act on one table.
- **DELETE** – Used to remove previously inserted rows from a table. The command can remove a single row or multiple rows from a table. When executed with no WHERE clause, it will remove all rows from the target table. It is not possible to delete individual columns – the entire row is deleted or it is not.
- **MERGE** – Used for hybrid DML operations. The MERGE can insert, update and delete rows in a table all in a single statement. There is no operation that a MERGE can perform that could not be performed by a combination of INSERT, UPDATE and DELETE.

Data control language

DCL statements are used to control access to data stored in a database. These access rights are maintained as a set of privileges stored in the data dictionary. The specific details of how privileges are maintained in a relational database are not an industry standard. Therefore, these details will change from one vendor to another.

It is notable that while this exam breaks out Data Control Language (DCL) statement into a separate category – in reality they are simply a subset of DDL commands. Since user privileges are information that is stored in the data dictionary, any commands that alter those privileges change the dictionary and are therefore DDL.

By default, objects that are created by one database user are not accessible by other users unless those users have special administrative rights. This means that in order for USER_A to access tables that are owned by USER_B, USER_A must have been granted access to do so. This might happen if USER_A were granted a system-wide privilege such as SELECT ANY TABLE. Alternately, USER_A might have been specifically granted privileges on the table by USER_B, or by another user that has privileges that allow them to grant the required access. Until a privilege has been granted, a relational database will generally treat attempts to SELECT from it as if the table does not even exist.

```
SELECT *
FROM   hr.regions;

ORA-00942: table or view does not exist
00942. 00000 -  "table or view does not exist"
*Cause:
*Action:
```

The three commands available in the Data Control Language are GRANT, REVOKE and DENY. All three will be discussed in Domain 4.4.

1.3 Identify relational data modeling schemas, characteristics and manipulation

Data abstraction in relational databases

Data abstraction is a means for representing data in such a way that the implementation details are hidden. This is done by removing specific details in order to reduce it to a set of essential characteristics. For example, when a user queries rows from the EMPLOYEES table, there is no need for him to be aware of the file name in the operating system that the data is coming from. There are three levels of data abstraction:

Physical, Conceptual, and External. They are also referred to as the Physical schema, Conceptual schema, and External schema.

Physical Data Level

The physical data level is the details of exactly how data is stored at the operating system level. Essentially it names the specific files where data and indexes and other database elements are stored on a physical drive. It generally also includes a description of the record layout of files and type of indexes (hash, b-tree, bitmap). Early database applications worked at the physical level and explicitly dealt with details of the data storage. However, working at the physical level introduces a number of problems.

- Routines must be hard coded to work with the physical representation.
- It is difficult to make changes to data structures.
- The application code must be more complex in order to deal with the details of the physical storage.
- It is difficult to implement new features rapidly.

Conceptual Data Level

The Conceptual data level is sometimes referred to as the Logical level. The conceptual data level hides the details of the physical level. In relational databases, the conceptual schema presents data as a set of tables. All mapping between the conceptual and physical schemas is performed automatically by the DBMS. There is no need for users or applications to be aware of the physical location of data in order to read or write from a given table in the database. Because this mapping is performed automatically, it is possible to change aspects at the physical level without impacting database applications. For example a table could be moved from one file to another or split among two files. The DBMS will handle the logical-to-physical mapping changes automatically. Because applications are written to the logical level, they will not be impacted. This is referred to as physical data independence.

External Data Level

The external data level is how data is actually viewed by users. This is likely to be simplified even further than the conceptual level. The external schema tailors the data to the needs of the users who are accessing it. For example, employees of a company might be able to view portions of the personnel database such as name, office location and phone number. However, most employees should not be able to view confidential information about others such as social security number or salary. However, if the employee viewing the data is a member of the Human Resources department, they should be able to access confidential data. The translation from the external to conceptual levels is performed automatically by the DBMS at run time. This allows the conceptual schema to be changed without impacting what is seen at the external level. This is referred to as conceptual data independence.

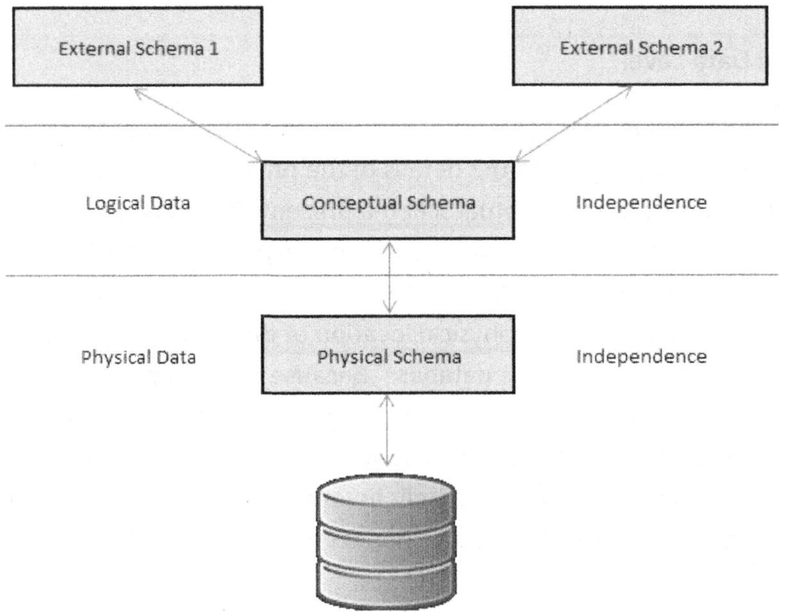

Multitier database architecture

The first computerized databases were developed during the age of mainframe computing. This necessitated a single-tier model also known as Centralized DBMS Architecture. In a centralized database, all of the database functionality: data, application code, and user interface processing is handled by a single machine. In the 1970s, mainframe computers were the only systems in widespread use. All of the database software was located on the mainframe and users interacted with it via dumb terminals. The terminals had effectively no processing power. Dumb terminals are primarily a keyboard, screen, and the capability to send data to and receive data from the mainframe. The Database Management System was completely centralized, with the dumb terminals performing no actions beyond accepting commands from users and displaying results from the mainframe. A major problem with this model is that the ability of the dumb terminals to provide a 'friendly' user interface was very limited. The need for the mainframe to perform all of the processing meant that dumb terminals were limited to a text-only interface.

In the 1980s, the rise of personal computers led to a change in the way processing took place. Unlike dumb terminals, PCs have the processing capacity to perform more tasks than simply send and receive data. With PCs acting as clients, more sophisticated software could run at the client workstation. This allowed for both more complex user interfaces -- such as Graphical User Interfaces (GUIs) as well as the ability to perform some processing at the client-side rather than having everything be performed at the central location (the server in client-server architecture). Because the client performs some of the processing, the processing requirements of the server are reduced. This allows for either a less powerful machine or one that spends more of its processing power on operations specific to the DBMS rather than interactions with users.

The Internet first came into its own in the late 1990s, and the client-server model fit in well with this. When the client and server are connected via an internal network such as Ethernet, the client-server architecture is normally implemented using a two-tier model, where the clients directly communicate with the database server. However, client-server architecture can be implemented as a three-tier model as well. In this model, the client communicates with an application server, which in turn communicates with the database server. The three-tier model is commonly used for web-based applications where the middle tier acts as the web server. The web server accepts requests from the clients and passes them to the databases server. The database server processes the requests and passes them back to the web server which in turn provides them to the client. Web-based database clients made it easier for organizations to provide widespread access to databases for either their employees or their customers.

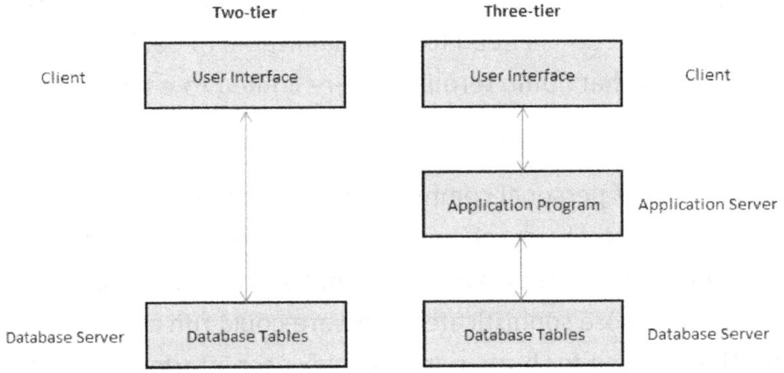

The workload differences between the two-tier and three-tier models are:

Two-tier client-server architecture

- **Client** -- user interface, business and data processing logic
- **Database server** -- data validation and database access

Three-tier client-server architecture

- **Client** -- user interface
- **Application server** -- business and processing logic
- **Database server** -- data validation and database access

There are two broad classes of clients that can be utilized in a multi-tier architecture:

- **Fat-Client** -- A fat client is a computer in client–server architecture that provides significant functionality independent of what is provided by the centralized server. A fat client requires at least periodic connection to a the central server, but can perform many functions without making use of the connection.
- **Thin-client** -- A thin client is a computer in a multi-tier client architecture that provides minimal functionality independent of what is provided by the centralized server. One of the most common thin-clients is a Web browser. Regardless of the slecific client, they generally server to accept user input that will then be processed on another computer (the server) which will then send result back to the thin-client for display. In many ways thin clients act much like dumb terminals.

Relational model terminology

A relation is a mathematical element in relational algebra. When writing relational algebra, a relation is the symbol ‘r’. Instances and schemas are likewise elements of relational algebra. The definitions are useful to know primarily because as a developer you may encounter these terms. While most developers do not tend to use relational algebra terms in general (certainly I do not), they show up occasionally in documentation and other sources. The following terms are required to understand how instances and schemas fit into relational algebra:

- **Tuple** – A tuple is a single element of a relation. In database terms, it is a row. A tuple is represented by the letter 't' in relational algebra.
- **Relation** – A relation is a set of unique tuples. The letter 'r' is used to represent a relation.
- **Attribute** – An attribute is equivalent to a column in a table. It is an element that qualifies, quantifies or describes an entity.
- **Attribute Value** – This is a value stored in an attribute. For an entity containing Customer data, an attribute might be 'First Name' and an attribute value 'John.'
- **Domain** – A domain is equivalent to a column data type and any constraints on the values of that data. For example the 'First Name' of a customer field would be character data and might have a restriction that it not be NULL.
- **Relation schema** – This element represents the name and the structure of the relation. The symbol used in relational algebra for this is 'R'.
- **Relation instance** -- The instance of a relation schema can be thought of as a table with n columns and one or more rows. In relational algebra, r(R) is used to represent a relation instance (with r being the rows and R being the table definition).
- **Relational database schema** – This is a collection of relation schemas.
- **Degree** – Number of attributes in a relation.
- **Cardinality** – Number of tuples in a relation.

On the (hopefully rare) occasions when people refer to a table in terms of relational algebra, they will sometimes use the term 'relation' when they are actually referring to a 'relation instance'. Seldom is it really useful in database terms to think of the set of rows in a table as being separate from the table structure they are stored in. The below diagram shows all of the individual elements of a relation instance.

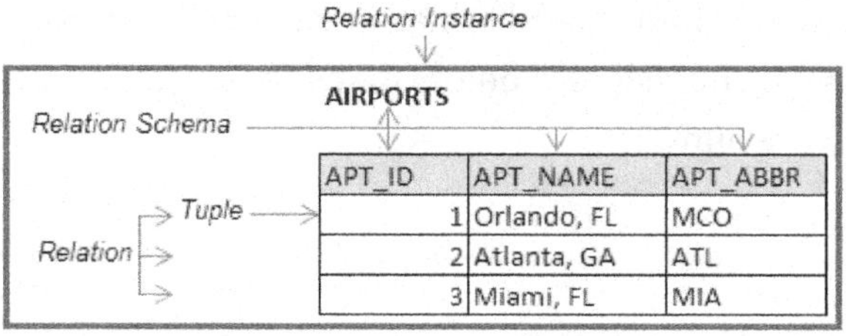

You should be aware that there is another term that includes the word 'instance' that you may encounter besides a relation instance. A relation instance is part of relational algebra, but there is a term called an entity instance that is part of the language of Entity Relationship Diagrams (ERDs). An instance in this model is a single occurrence of the entity type being tracked. For example, given the Airport entity in the diagram below, one instance would be Orlando International Airport (MCO) in Orlando, Florida. An entity instance corresponds to a row in the physical database model.

- **Entity** – An entity is a grouping of things with rules or data in common.
- **Entity instance** -- An entity instance is a single occurrence of an entity.

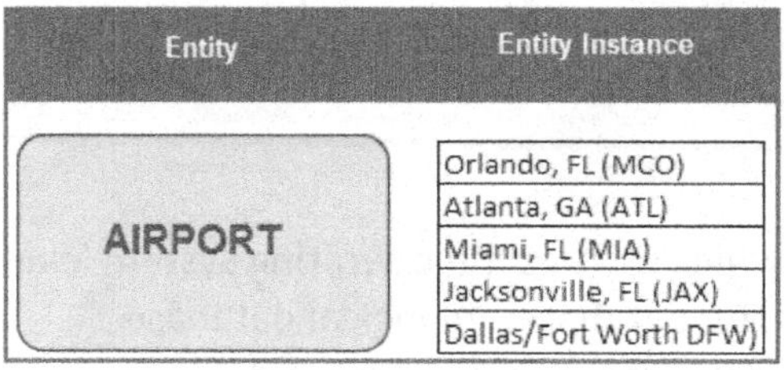

On the test (and in the real world) you may see a number of different terms used for the same database elements depending on what setting they are in. Unfortunately, in some cases the terms have become interchangeable so that you might see terms used in the wrong setting.

You should be aware that rows, columns, and tables in particular can be referred to by different names. The diagram below maps these names to three variants that you may encounter.

File System	Relational Algebra	Analysis/Design	Physical
Records	Tuples	Instances	Rows
Fields	Attributes	Attributes	Columns
Files	Relations	Entities	Tables

There are people in this world (I am not one of them) who get upset when people refer to columns in a relational database table as 'fields', or rows as 'records'. It is certainly not something that I obsess over, but ideally you should refer to items by the correct name.

Data storage in the relational model

An important characteristic of a relational database is that physical storage structures are independent of logical data structures. Because the two are kept separate, it is possible to administer the physical storage of data without affecting the logical structures that are contained within them. Some of the database storage elements common to all RDBMS systems include:

- **Data files** (Physical) -- Data files exist at the operating system level and contain all the data of the database. All logical database structures, such as tables and indexes, are stored in data files.
- **Table** (Logical) -– Tables are the primary logical element in relational databases and contain the information which is manipulated via SQL. A table contains a collection of closely related columns and consists of rows which share the same columns but vary in the column values.

- **Index** (Logical) -- Indexes are a data structure associated with tables that can improve the speed of data retrieval operations at the cost of additional writes and storage.
- **Column** (Logical) -– A single unit of named data that has a particular data type. Columns only exist in tables.
- **Row** (Logical) -– One set of related values for all of the columns declared in a given table.

The RDBMS that I am most familiar with is Oracle. There are a number of storage structures in the Oracle database beyond those mentioned above. Since not all of these exist in other databases, the test will likely not cover them. However, I have included them here in any event for completeness:

- **Control files** (Physical) -– Control files contains information specifying the physical structure of the database, including the database name and the names and locations of the database files.
- **Online redo log files** (Physical) -– A set of two or more online redo log files makes up an online redo log. An online redo log contains redo entries which record all changes made to data in the database.
- **Data blocks** (Logical) -– At the finest level of granularity, data is stored in data blocks. One data block corresponds to a specific number of bytes on disk.
- **Extents** (Logical) -– An extent is a specific number of logically contiguous data blocks, obtained in a single allocation, and used to store a specific type of information.
- **Segments** (Logical) -– A segment is a set of extents allocated for a user object (for example, a table or index), undo data, or temporary data.
- **Tablespaces** (Logical) -– A database is divided into logical storage units called tablespaces. A tablespace is the logical container for a segment.

Data models

When starting the process of designing the architecture of a database, developers generally begin with a conceptual model to get a very high-level feel for the basic data elements to be stored. Additional information is then added to the conceptual model to form a logical model of the data. When the developer (or development team) is confident that the data to be stored and relationships are correct, the logical model is used to construct a physical model. The level and types of information contained in conceptual, logical, and physical models is summarized in the following table:

Feature	Conceptual	Logical	Physical
Entity Names	✓	✓	
Entity Relationships	✓	✓	
Attributes		✓	
Primary Keys		✓	✓
Foreign Keys		✓	✓
Table Names			✓
Column Names			✓
Column Data Types			✓

Earlier in this guide, three tables from the Imaginary Airlines database were introduced: AIRPORTS, AIRCRAFT_TYPES, and AIRCRAFT_FLEET. The following diagrams illustrate how these entities would appear in each of the three models:

Conceptual

Logical

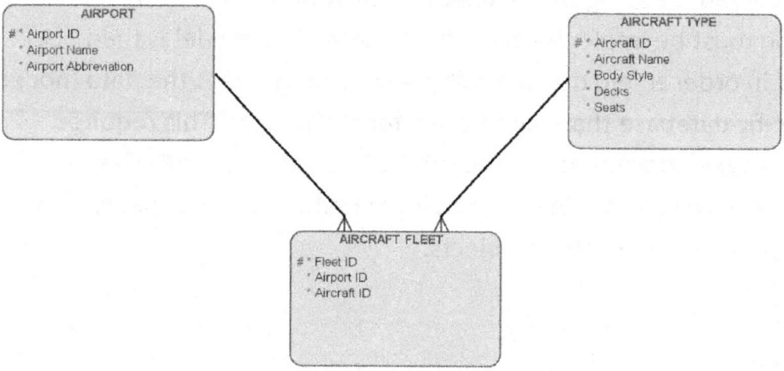

Physical

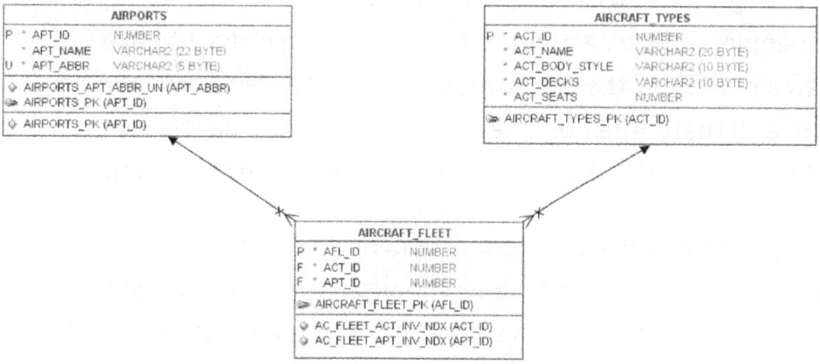

The examples above clearly demonstrate the increasing level of complexity from conceptual to logical to physical. Starting with the conceptual data model makes it easier for the developer (and the users supplying requirements) to understand at a very high level what the different data entities are and how they relate to each other. For example, there is no reason for business users to understand the need for breaking out the AIRCRAFT FLEET entity. From the user viewpoint, aircraft are based at airports, so two only entities need to be represented.

The logical data model is useful for illustrating the types of data that must be tracked without having to consider exactly how storage of this information must be implemented. The physical data model is then developed in order to pin down exactly how to implement the data model in the specific database that will be used for the project. This requires picking data type appropriate to the RDBMS that will be used. The physical model will be the final step before creating the SQL that will be used to construct the database objects.

Entities and data relationships

An entity is a grouping of things (or a class of things) with rules or data in common. Among other possibilities, an entity might be used to represent a group of people, objects, activities, or concepts. In order to have relevance to a database, the entity must have some significance to an organization and there must be a requirement to store data about it. When implementing a database -- an entity corresponds to a table.

For Imaginary Airlines, airports are an important element to their business. An entity that stores data about airports is therefore something that would need to be included in a database application for the organization. In the conceptual model, an entity is shown as simply a rectangle with the name of the entity either inside or sometimes just above the rectangle.

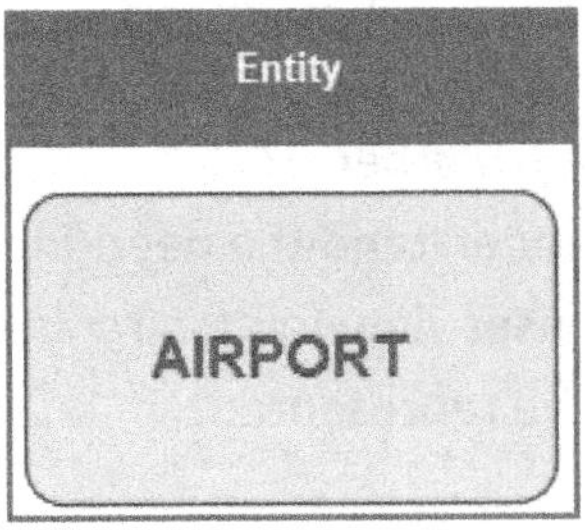

Database developers should recognize that while an entity corresponds to a table, it is not the exactly same thing. An entity is an object in the real world with an independent existence. Examples of potential entities include:

- An object with physical existence (such as an airport or an aircraft).
- An object with conceptual existence (such as a flight or a ticket reservation).

Entities are the primary component of Entity Relationship Diagrams (ERDs). ERDs (which will be discussed in greater detail in later chapters) are used as a design aid when developing database applications. Below is a conceptual model ERD that contains three entities. It should be obvious that they correspond to the three Imaginary Airlines tables that have appeared in previous chapters. However, the conceptual model contains no specifics. Conceptual models are only intended to show a very high-level overview of the various entities that must be contained in the database and a basic idea of the relationships between entities. It does not provide specific details of the data that will be stored.

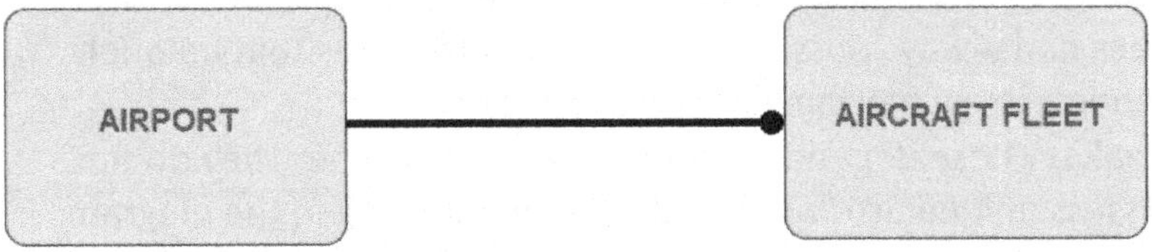

Likewise, the relationships shown between the entities have no details. In the diagram, it is possible to determine that there is a relationship between the AIRPORT and AIRCRAFT FLEET entities, but not what the relationship is based on. If the diagram were displaying tables rather than entities, each of the tables would need to show all of the columns they contain as well as indicating which columns were acting as primary and foreign keys.

Because entities generally represent objects, their names are usually nouns. By convention, in an ERD, entity names are singular (AIRPORT rather than AIRPORTS) and they will be capitalized in the ERD.

Be aware that just because something is an object with a physical existence does not mean that it would be a candidate for an entity. One of the more common tables in a relational database, for example is one to hold employee data. An entity called EMPLOYEE would therefore make sense. However, if 'John Smith' is an employee of this company, it would not make sense to have an entity called JOHN SMITH. Entities represent a class of items that share common characteristics. The only thing that a 'JOHN SMITH' entity would logically contain is multiple occurrences of people named 'John Smith'. While it is certain that there are multiple people in the world with this name, it is harder to justify any reason for creating a dedicated database table to store information about them.

Conceptual and logical models will always have components to represent the entities involved in the model as well as connectors between the entities that represent the relationships. Entities are objects or concepts that represent critical data. There are three potential types of entities:

- **Strong** -- These entities exist independently from other entity types and always possess one or more attributes that uniquely distinguish each occurrence of the entity.
- **Weak** -- These depend on some other entity type. They do not possess unique attributes and have no meaning in the diagram without depending on another entity.
- **Associative** -- These are entities that associate the instances of one or more entity types.

There are specific shapes that can be used in an ERD to represent each of the three entity types:

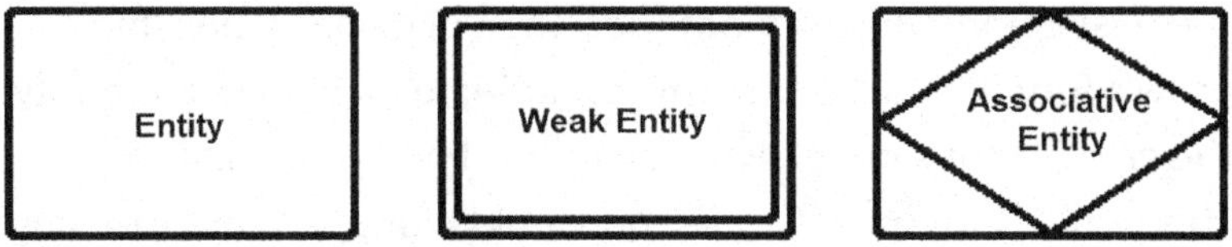

Data relationships

Data relationships illustrate the association between two entities in the model. In the conceptual data model, the lines representing relationships are generally nothing more than a simple line connecting the two entities. In the logical and physical data models, relationships are typically represented by stylized lines that provide the view with details about the relationship such as cardinality and ordinality. I have occasionally seen conceptual models that utilize these stylized representations, but generally this is not the case. The below diagram is a conceptual model diagram where the bare line indicates that a data relationship exists, but provides no hint as to the details of the relationship.

Cardinality and Ordinality

Cardinality and ordinality are two pieces of information about data relationships that can be indicated graphically via the styling of the line and its endpoint.

- **Cardinality** -- Refers to the maximum number of times an instance in one entity can be associated with instances in a related entity.
- **Ordinality** -- Refers to the minimum number of times an instance in one entity can be associated with an instance in a related entity.

Probably the most commonly used notation seen in data relationships is called the crow's foot. It indicates 'many' or multiple records in the entity closest to the crow's foot symbol. For example, a line connecting two entities with a crow's foot on only one end would indicate a one-to-many relationship, while a line with a crow's foot on both ends would indicate a many-to-many relationship. The following diagram shows a number of different symbols that can be used to indicate cardinality and ordinality in a data model:

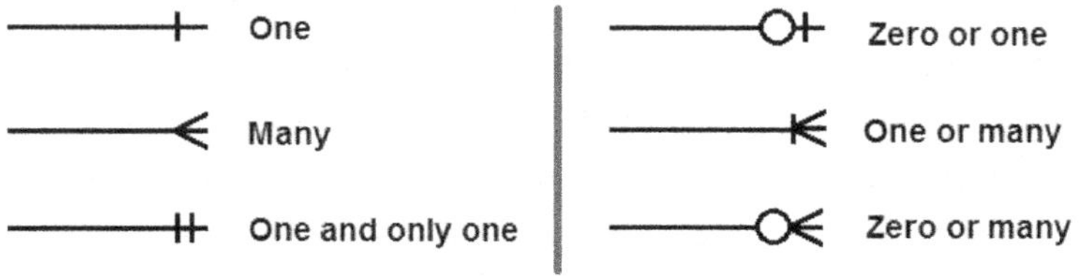

The above set is only one of a number of different ERD notation styles that can be used to indicate the cardinality and ordinality that exists between two entities. Some of the possible cardinality combinations are detailed in the following table:

Left	Right	Cardinality	Example
1	1	One-to-one	Aircraft <-> Electrical System
0..1	1	Optional on one side one-to-one	Flight e-ticket <-> Flight Reservation
0..* or *	1..* or *	Optional on one side many-to-many	Flight Survey <-> Aircraft Flight
1..* or *	1..* or *	Many-to-many	Airline Customer <-> Aircraft Flight
1	0..*	Optional on one side one-to-many	Airport <-> Aircraft Fleet
1	1..*	One-to-many	Airline Customer <-> Flight Reservation

Using the second line from the top in the illustration above – a flight reservation will always have one and only one ticket. However, it is possible to have a flight reservation for which the customer uses a printed ticket rather than an e-ticket. The two entities therefore have a one-to-one relationship, but it is possible no e-ticket instance exists for a given flight reservation. Therefore the relationship is optional on the e-ticket side and can be zero.

Using the bottom line of the above illustration, an airline customer can have multiple reservations, and it is impossible for a reservation to exist without an associated customer record. A person will not exist in the Airline Customers table until they have made their first flight reservation. The two entities therefore have a one-to-many relationship that is not optional on either side.

If two entities in an ERD have a relationship (for example entity A and entity B) there will always be an expectation of how many instances in A relate to how many instances in B. There are only three possibilities:

- **One-to-one** -- A single instance in A will never relate to more than a single instance in B.
- **One-to-many** -- A single instance in A can relate to one or more instances in B.
- **Many-to-many** -- Multiple instances in A can relate to multiple instances in B.

On an ER diagram, there are actually <u>four</u> different notations to represent the above <u>three</u> possibilities because the one-to-many is broken out by direction:

- **1:1** -- one-to-one
- **1:N** -- one-to-many
- **M:1** -- many-to-one
- **M:N** -- many-to-many

One-to-one relationships are fairly rare in the real world. As a general rule, if there is a one-to-one relationship between two entities, the attributes often make more sense stored in a single entity. A one-to-one example using the Imaginary Airlines model might be entities which stored information about separate systems of individual aircraft in the IA fleet. There might be one table for electrical systems, another for emergency systems, and another for cabin fixtures. Each of these would have a one-to-one relationship with the Aircraft Fleet entity (which has a single instance for each aircraft). This allows Imaginary Airlines to keep the information about each aircraft system separate while ensuring that the information for each individual aircraft is maintained.

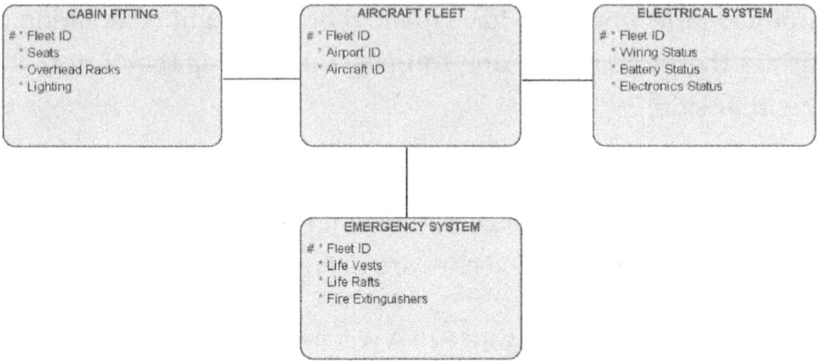

One-to-many relationships are by far the most common type encountered in the real world. The diagram below of the Airports and Aircraft Fleet entities has a one-to-many relationship. Multiple aircraft in the Imaginary Airlines fleet can be based out of a given airport. However, each individual aircraft can have only one home airport. Therefore each instance in the Airport entity has a one-to-many relationship with the Aircraft Fleet entity.

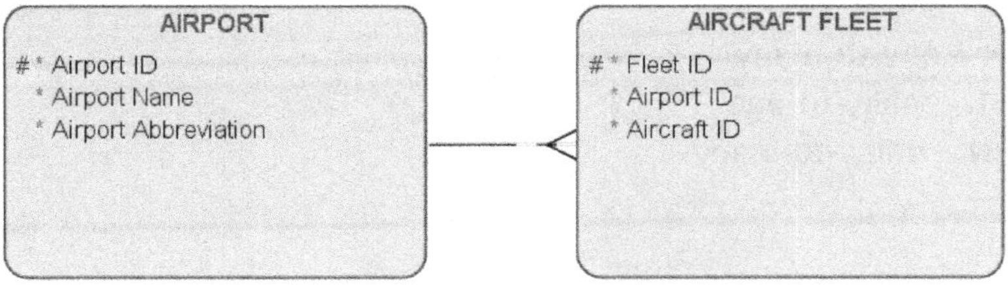

Many-to-many relationships come in between the previous two in terms of how commonly they are seen in the real world. Many-to-many relationships between two entities are implemented by creating a third entity called an intersection entity. Each of the original two entities has a one-to-many relationship with the intersection entity. This in turn gives them a many-to-many relationship when viewed across both relationships. The intersection entity often has no reason for existence other than providing this link. In the Imaginary Airlines schema, the Airline Customers and Aircraft Flights entities have a many-to-many relationship. One customer can take many flights with Imaginary Airlines and each flight will (hopefully) contain multiple customers. In the example below, the intersection entity is Flight Reservations. In addition to facilitating the many-to-many link between Airline Customers and Aircraft Flights, this intersection entity can contain information about the reservation such as the price, date of purchase, etc.

Optionality

Another aspect of data relationships is optionality. The two possible values for the optionality of a relationship are:

- **Mandatory Relationship** -- A mandatory relationship specifies that each instance from an entity must be related to another instance. This is represented by a straight line.
- **Optional Relationship** -- An optional relationship specifies that each instance from an entity may be related to another instance. This is represented by a dashed line.

An example of a mandatory relationship would be that every aircraft in the Imaginary Airlines fleet must have cabin fittings, an electrical system, and an emergency system. It would not make sense for an aircraft to be missing any of these systems. None of these are optional for the aircraft.

The following diagram depicts this non-optional one-to-one relationship among the four entities.

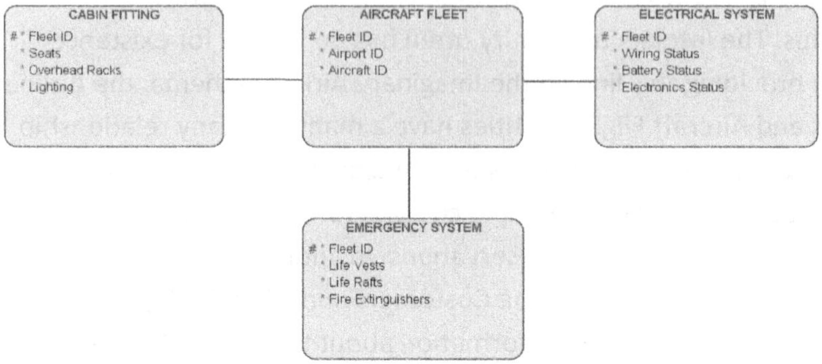

By contrast, an example of an optional relationship would be whether Imaginary Airlines has one or more of its fleet of aircraft based out of a given airport. The right-hand portion of the line is dashed, indicating that the relationship is optional from the Aircraft Fleet side while being mandatory from the Airport side. A given instance in the Airport entity does not have to be the home for one or more aircraft in the Imaginary Airlines fleet. Imaginary Airlines may fly to many different airports that it does not store aircraft at for extended periods. However, if an instance exists in the Aircraft Fleet, that aircraft <u>must</u> have a home airport. The relationship is therefore optional only from one direction.

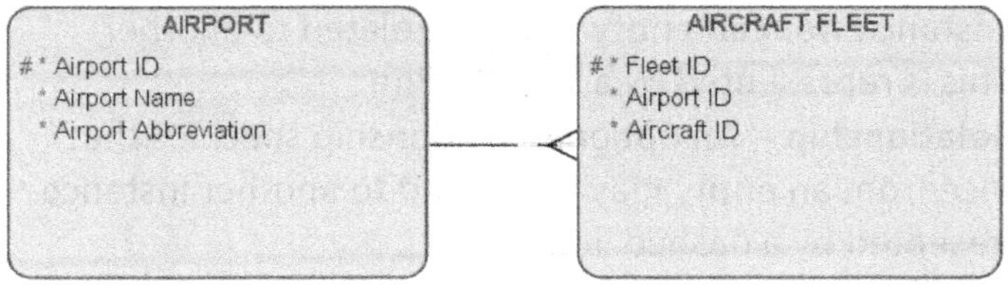

Transferability

A relationship is nontransferable if an instance of entity A is related to an instance of entity B, and the association cannot be moved to a different instance of B. If the association can be moved, the relationship is transferable. Generally the business rules of the organization will determine whether or not a relationship can be transferred.

For example, in the Imaginary Airline schema, the Airline Customer entity has a one-to-many relationship with the Flight Reservation entity. A given customer may have purchased tickets for one flight or several. If the policy of Imaginary Airlines is that tickets can be transferred to another customer once purchased, the relationship is transferrable and would be represented with the normal relationship notation as shown in the diagram below.

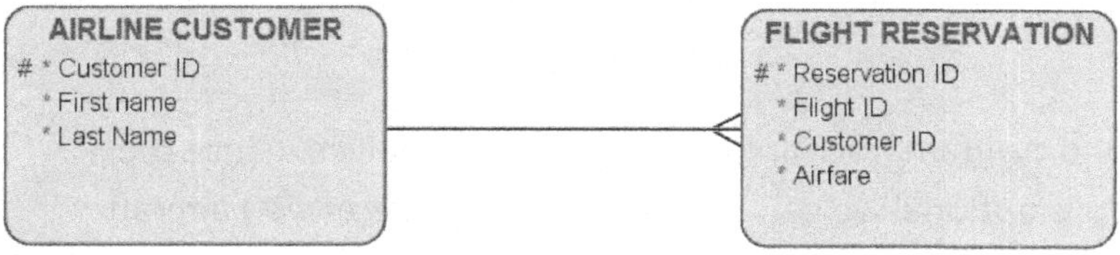

However, if the Imaginary Airlines policy is that tickets, once purchased, can be cancelled but never transferred to a different customer, then the relationship between the two entities is nontransferable. In this case, the relationship between the two would have a diamond symbol to indicate that the relationship cannot be transferred.

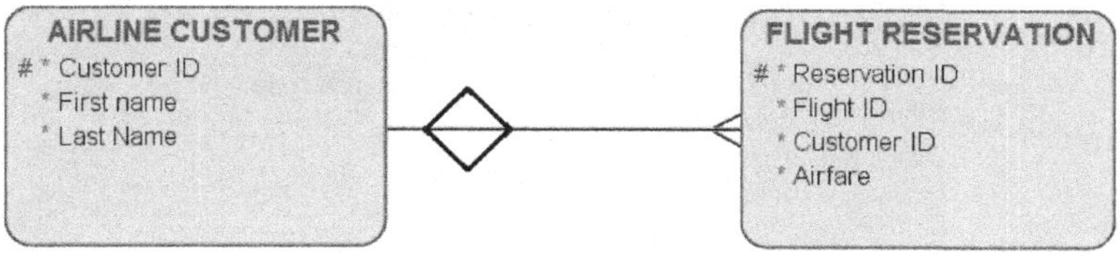

Named Relationships

Named relationships have an additional component to them that makes the specific link between two entities clearer. Because relationships must be viewed from both sides, named relationships have one name for each side to show the different viewpoints. For example, the first diagram below has '*purchased*' on the 'Airline Customer' side of the relationship, but '*purchased by*' on the Flight Reservation side. An airline customer has purchased a flight reservation whereas a flight reservation is purchased by an airline customer.

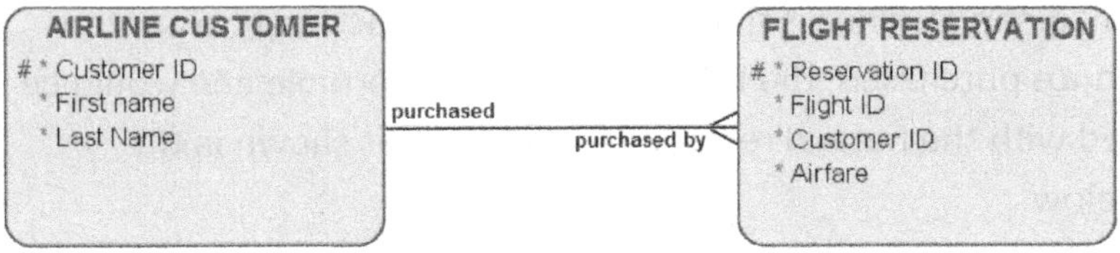

In the second diagram, the Aircraft Fleet entity *'received'* (since the relationship is optional we can also say *'may have received'*) aircraft maintenance performed on it. Personally, I hope that any plane I fly on 'has received' maintenance at some point fairly recently. From the other side the relationship is mandatory since a maintenance record cannot exist without an aircraft. From that viewpoint, the statement can only be aircraft maintenance *'has been performed on'* an instance of the aircraft fleet.

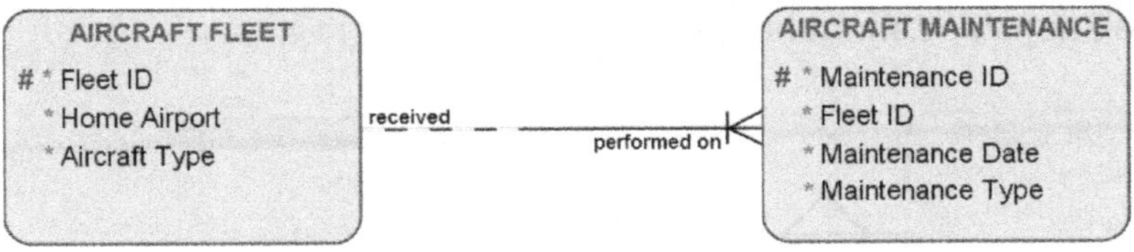

Hierarchical

A hierarchical relationship is a series of relationships that reflect entities organized into successive levels. Each child entity instance is able to store a reference to a single parent entity instance. The parent entity instance can be referenced by an unlimited number of child entity instances. A one-to-many relationship is hierarchical when viewed from the primary entity. Any one entity instance from the parent entity can be referenced by many instances from the child entity.

Hierarchical relationships occur commonly in the real world. Organizational charts are one of the most common examples. The parts for complex pieces of equipment are often formed into hierarchies. Family trees make up a hierarchy.

In the Imaginary Airlines schema a hierarchical relationship between entities can be demonstrated with the AIRPORT, AIRCRAFT FLEET, AIRCRAFT FLIGHT, and FLIGHT RESERVATION entities. A given airport can be the home site for several instances of the AIRCRAFT FLEET. Each instance of the AIRCRAFT FLEET can make multiple flights. Each flight will have multiple reservations. This is illustrated in the diagram below:

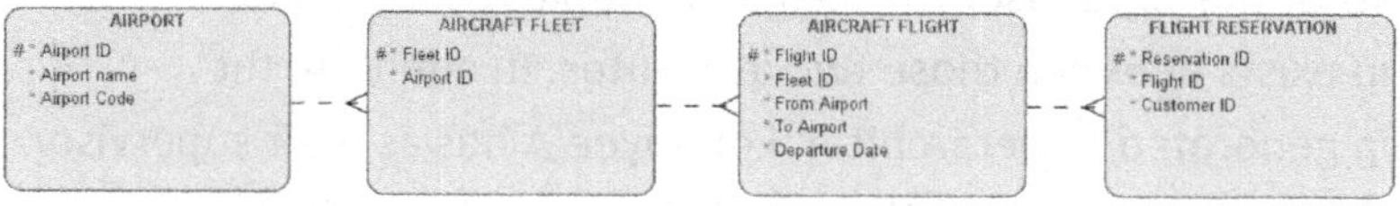

Recursive

A recursive relationship occurs when there is relationship between an entity and itself. This can happen when one of the attributes in an entity references the unique identifier column of the entity. In the Imaginary Airlines schema, one of the entities is AIRCRAFT MAINT. It stores all of the maintenance records for each aircraft in the fleet. While employees are performing maintenance, sometimes they will identify a need to perform a separate maintenance action that is outside their job role. For example, while working on a problem with the wing flaps, a technician might identify a problem with one of the engines. A new instance in the AIRCRAFT MAINT entity will be created to track the required maintenance. The second problem was identified by the first and the entity has an attribute to store this 'parent' maintenance instance. A recursive relationship can therefore be made between the AIRCRAFT MAINT entity and itself as per the below diagram:

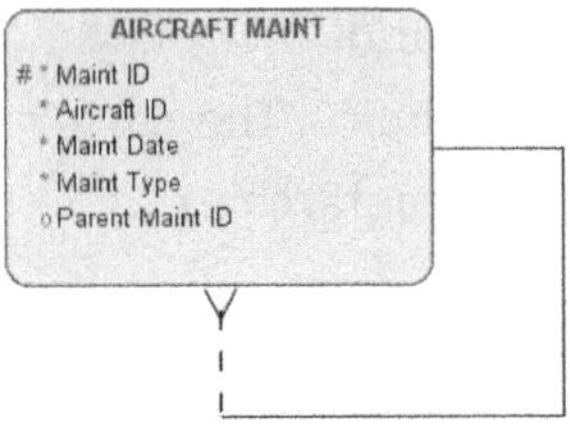

One of the most common examples of a recursive relationship is an entity that stores employee data. One attribute might be used for the employee ID number of the current instance while a second attribute stores the employee ID of the supervisor for the given employee. A recursive relationship exists between those two attributes. In addition, the relationship generated is hierarchical. Employee A has as their supervisor employee B. Employee B has as their supervisor Employee C, and so on, right up to the highest level employee (who will have a NULL value in the Supervisor ID field). When a database has an employee table with these two fields, it is commonly used to generate hierarchical queries that return organizational charts for the business.

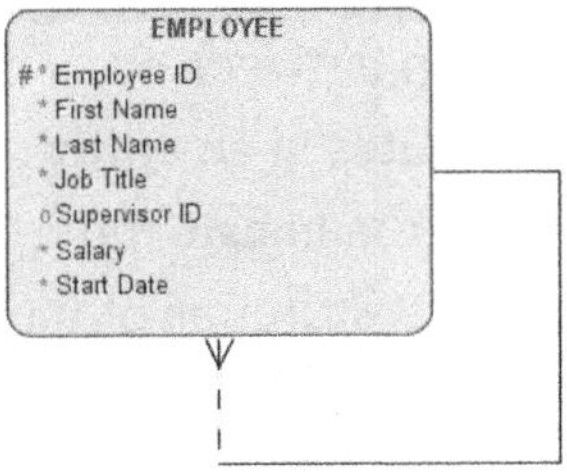

Relational integrity

Relational integrity, also known as referential integrity, is a concept designed to ensure that the information that relates one table to another follows a given set of guidelines. These guidelines are determined by the database design and by the business rules of the organization using the database. When working with a relational database, it is expected that data in related tables should always stay related. For example, flights booked for a given aircraft should never be confused with flights booked for a different aircraft. The RDBMS mechanisms that are used to maintain data integrity are called constraints. Constraints are database objects that are used to restrict (constrain) the data allowed into table columns. They are essentially rules that must be met in order for a value to be acceptable. There are several different kinds of constraints available in relational databases including:

- **PRIMARY KEY** – The primary key of a table is used to ensure entity integrity. It defines a column, or set of columns that must be unique for every row of a table. To satisfy a primary key constraint, none of the column(s) making up the key may be NULL, and the combination of values in the column(s) must be unique. A table can have only a single primary key constraint defined (all other constraint types can exist multiple times in the same table).
- **UNIQUE** – A unique key defines a column or set of columns that must be unique for every row of a table. Unlike a primary key constraint, the UNIQUE constraint does not prevent NULL values in the columns(s) comprising the constraint.
- **NOT NULL** – A NOT NULL constraint prevents a table column from having NULL values. If a column with a UNIQUE constraint is also defined as NOT NULL, it will have the same restrictive behavior as a PRIMARY KEY.
- **FOREIGN KEY** – Foreign keys are also referred to as Referential Integrity constraints. A foreign key constraint ties a column value in one table to a primary or unique key value in another. Values may not be inserted in the table with the reference constraint that do not exist in the referenced key.
- **CHECK** – Check constraints allow for custom conditions to be specified for a column. The conditions must evaluate to TRUE for

the operation altering the column value to succeed. Check constraints are often used to maintain domain integrity, such as ensuring data has valid values, length, formatting, and so forth.

Foreign Keys

If two tables contain one or more common columns, a foreign key can be used to enforce the relationship between the two tables. This enforced relationship is known as referential integrity. For this reason, foreign key constraints are also called referential integrity constraints. When a foreign key is in place, it requires that for each value in the column on which the constraint is defined, the equivalent value in the other table and column must match.

The below diagram shows data in the AIRPORTS, AIRCRAFT_TYPES and AIRCRAFT_FLEET tables. The AIRCRAFT_FLEET has one foreign key reference to AIRPORTS and a second to AIRCRAFT_TYPES. These constraints would prevent a row from being added to the AIRCRAFT_FLEET table that had a value of 10 in the APT_ID column because there is no corresponding row in the AIRPORTS table where the APT_ID column was equal to 10. The same logic would prevent the insertion of a row in AIRCRAFT_FLEET with an ACT_ID value of 8. Foreign key constraints essentially prevent 'garbage' data from entering the database.

The constraint does not apply only to data being added to the table. A SQL action that attempted to update a constrained column in an existing row to a non-existent value would also be prevented. The behavior on delete operations is a bit more complex. Delete operations on the AIRCRAFT_FLEET table would not be prevented by a foreign key constraint. However, deletes on the parent table when child records exist might be prevented depending on how the foreign key was defined.

AIRCRAFT FLEET

AFL_ID	ACT_ID	APT_ID
1	2	1
2	2	1
3	3	2
4	4	2
5	1	3
6	1	3
7	1	5
8	2	5

AIRPORTS

APT_ID	APT_NAME	APT_ABBR
1	Orlando, FL	MCO
2	Atlanta, GA	ATL
3	Miami, FL	MIA
4	Jacksonville, FL	JAX
5	Dallas/Fort Worth	DFW
7	Houston, TX	IAH

AIRCRAFT TYPES

ACT_ID	ACT_NAME	ACT_BODY	ACT_DECKS	ACT_SEATS
1	Boeing 747	Wide	Double	416
2	Boeing 767	Wide	Single	350
3	Boeing 737	Narrow	Single	200
4	Boeing 757	Narrow	Single	240
5	Boeing 777	Wide	Single	407
6	Boeing 787	Wide	Single	296

Data dictionaries

One of the most critical aspects of a relational database is its data dictionary. The data dictionary is a read-only set of tables that contain metadata about the database. A data dictionary contains all of the information about the database structure including:

- The definitions of every schema object in the database
- The amount of space allocated for and currently used by the schema objects
- The names of database users
- Privileges and roles granted to database users
- Auditing information

The data dictionary is a central part of how the Database Management System (DBMS) maintains and controls the system. The DBMS uses the data dictionary to perform many actions such as locating information about users, schema objects, and storage structures. Because the data dictionary data is itself stored in tables, database users can query the data using SQL. For example, it is possible to execute SELECT statements to locate the tables in a given database schema, list the columns in those tables. Queries against the data dictionary can locate all of the indexes in the database and what columns they reference.

Domain 2: Relational Database Design and Application

2.1 Identify the steps of the database planning life cycle

Introduction to database planning

Before the first entity is sketched out on paper and certainly before a single line of code is written, it is important to invest some time at the start of a database development project to creating a plan. When completed, this plan will serve as a guide to be used while developing the database as well as a functional specification for the system once completed. The complexity and detail of a database design is dictated by the complexity and size of the database application and also the user population. A database plan should include the following:

- **An executive summary** -- This will generally include a mission statement that clearly explains why a database is needed and what you the database is intended to accomplish.
- **Database design and information flow** -- This section identifies the data to be collected and stored by the database. it should also include the types of information and functionality that the collected data will be able to provide as a result.
- **Hardware/Software requirements** -- This section should identifies (or at least suggest) what additional hardware and/or software is required in order to implement the database.
- **Implementation plan** -- This is a schedule and/or deadline that indicates the timeline for developing the database and putting it into production. This should include the time spent collecting all data as well as completing the database development itself. In addition, the implementation plan should include a budget for all staff and hardware/software expenses required for the development process.

- **Security plan** -- Almost all databases require a security plan to ensure that access to see and modify data is available only to the intended individuals. Designing security into a database from the outset is much more effective than trying to add in security when the database nears completion.
- **Check-list for completion** -- Projects without a defined end-state are often subject to 'scope-creep' that pushes the end date further and further off. Creating a written end-state at the beginning of the project may not necessarily prevent this from occurring, but it can be invaluable to have as evidence if scope-creep causing the original deadlines to be missed.

Database design life cycle

Nothing lasts forever. The database being designed today to be implemented in a few months will be discarded at some point in the future when it gets replaced with something better. The database design lifecycle acknowledges the fact that this process is ongoing. There are many different variations for the database design lifecycle. Some display the steps in greater detail and others less. The model covered in this guide has five discrete steps, but you should not be surprised if the exam contains a lifecycle with four or six steps.

1. **Requirements Analysis** – This is essentially the planning covered in the previous chapter where the database developers and the organization work to create a written summary of what the database project is to accomplish and how.
2. **Logical Design** – This stage of the database design process consists of modeling the database at a logical level to map the data to be stored, the relationships between that data, and the information flow to the needs of the organization.
3. **Physical Design** – The logical design is converted into a design specific to a particular relational database. The entities, unique identifiers, relationships, and business rules are codified into tables, primary keys, foreign keys, and constraints.
4. **Implementation** – The database and its associated user interface are placed into production in the organization.

5. **Monitoring, Modification & Maintenance** – The database application receives ongoing attention while in production to ensure that it continues to serve the needs of the organization.

As the diagram below indicates, this is a cycle. Eventually, despite being maintained and modified while in production, the current system will no longer meet the needs of the organization. At that time, the process will start over again at step one with the requirements analysis for a replacement database.

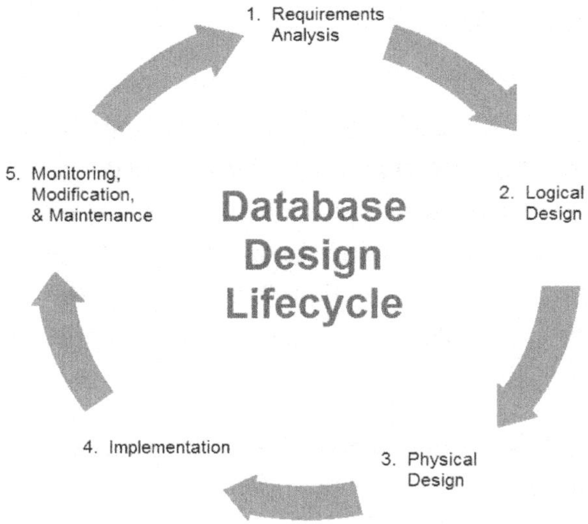

Gathering database requirements

One of the most difficult tasks in database development is obtaining all the requirements for the requested application. The process of gathering requirements is often frustrating enough that developers short-change it and start building the solution with insufficient information. The results of this are seldom optimal.

There are a number of techniques available for gathering information. Each can be useful, or not, depending on the specific circumstances involved in the project. In most cases, you will need to use two or more techniques to get a complete set of specifications for the solution to be developed. A well-designed database application should meet the following requirements:

- Stores all the data that needs to be tracked.
- Follows (or enforces) business rules for processing data.
- Protects data security and integrity.
- Is able to handle exceptions.
- Allows for growth and change.

One of the very first steps should be to create a statement of scope. This statement should clearly indicate, without getting into technical details, what information will be stored in the database and what the database application is intended to do. Once the statement exists, begin gathering requirements to design the new database solution. One or more of the following methods should be applicable to the vast majority of database development projects:

- **Review existing database** -- Seldom does the need for a new database application come out of nowhere. Generally there will be an existing system that is being replaced. The existing 'database' might be paper forms, spreadsheets, or an existing electronic database. Regardless of what exists, it provides a starting point that may allow developers to determine forms and reports that are currently used by the business for the task. Any new solution will generally need to provide a superset of the functionality that exists in the system being replaced.
- **One-on-one interviews** -- One of the most common methods for gathering requirements is to sit down with individuals who will be using the system to ask what they need from such a database. The developer must have a prepared list of questions to ask based on the type of requirements being sought. As a general rule, the questions asked should be open-ended in order to get the

interviewee to start talking and then follow those with more probing questions to uncover requirements.

- **Group interviews** -- The format for group interviews is similar to that of one-on-one interviews, except that more than one user is present -- usually two to four. Group interviews generally work best when all of the users have the same role. Group interviews generally require more preparation. However, the dynamics can sometimes results in obtaining more information than meeting with each of the users individually.
- **Questionnaires** -- Questionnaires are more informal than interviews and require much less time from the development team. They are particularly useful for gathering requirements from stakeholders in remote locations or those who will have only minor input into the system requirements. If there is a need to gather input from large numbers of people, questionnaires may be the only reasonable option. Questionnaires are best used for close ended questions such as determining technical information and facts.
- **Observation** -- Observing how people actually work with the data can be very useful in many cases. Users often perform their work routines so unconsciously that they have a hard time explaining what they do or why. This technique can help developers to see how they use the data, which data they use most, and the sequence in which they use it. This can make it more obvious how processes that currently take large amounts of time can be made more efficient through automation.
- **Prototyping** -- Many development environments today allow for rapid application development. Using this, it is possible to gather preliminary requirements and build an initial version of the solution. This solution is demonstrated to the client, who then provides additional requirements. The prototype is altered to the new requirements and demonstrated again. This process continues until the product meets the business needs. Prototyping can work, but it is definitely a resource-intensive method of gathering requirements.

Business Rules

A business rule is a statement that describes a business policy or procedure. When considered in terms of database application design, they represent conditions that the database application must enforce. Business rules are a significant part of the information that must be determined during the requirements gathering process. They are often one of the more difficult parts to pin down because the users often 'internalize' these requirements and will not think about them when asked about the required functionality of a database application.

Business rules must be coded in to database applications because they generally involve actions that are perfectly acceptable from a databases standpoint. For example, it is well-known that the Chik-fil-a fast food chain is closed on Sundays. A business rule for an application written for that company might well be that it will not function from 12:00 A.M. to midnight on Sundays. There is no technical reason why the database could not function during those hours, but the business rule must be met.

A more reasonable set of rules might involve restrictions for a database application created for a company's shipping department. The company has a number of policies in place about shipments, including:

- Shipments are only made on weekdays during the hours of 8:00 A.M. to 6:00 P.M.
- A single shipment can contain ten items or less
- A shipment cannot weigh more than fifty pounds.
- They only ship to addresses in the continental United States.

If the shipping database for this company allowed an order to be created with fifteen items weighing 100 pounds to be shipped to Australia on Saturday at 8:00 P.M., then there is a serious application failure. Business rules are very important to the proper functioning of a database application. Because they are often missed during the requirements gathering phase, special effort should be made to obtain this information.

Selecting the RDBMS

There are a number of options to choose from when deciding on a specific RDBMS to host the database being developed. It is virtually certain that any RDBMS will have the base capability to host the table structure that will be developed during the conceptual and logical design phases. Where the platforms of various vendors differ is in the capabilities they provide beyond that of simply allowing for the creating of tables, indexes, constraints, etc. in a relational model. Some of the areas in which database vendors will differ include the following:

- Performance
- Reliability
- Scalability
- Manageability
- Security
- Concurrency
- Transaction Control
- Backup and Restore Capabilities
- High Availability
- Development Tools
- Support for data compression and encryption
- Data Types available
- Data integrity support
- Available interfaces
- Utilities and admin tools
- Cost
- Technical Support Availability
- Reputation
- Documentation

Once a given database application has been designed and built on a given RDBMS, moving it to a different one is a major undertaking. A significant percentage, (quite possibly the majority) of the application will have to be rewritten from scratch. Therefore, it is very important to carefully consider which RDBMS to utilize. The first four factors in the above list are some of the most critical when picking a database platform. That is not to indicate the other factors are not also important, but it is worth expanding on the first set.

- **Performance** -- No one ever complains that the response time of a database application is just too darn fast. On the other hand, complaints about operations that take too long are common. It simply does not matter how well designed a database application is or how much functionality it provides if the users feel that working with it is too slow. Unfortunately, performance is something that is very difficult to gauge while developing a database application. Many performance problems will not appear until the database contains a sufficiently large number of records. You do not want to find out that a given application works with amazing speed when it has an initial 1,000 test records, then very fast when it has 100,000 records, then acceptably quick with 1,000,000 records but dog slow once there are 10,000,000 records in place.
- **Reliability** -- An RDBMS must be reliable enough that critical applications can proceed with normal operations at all times. Enterprise-class relational database software will provide capabilities that protect data at multiple levels. There will be options for protecting data that resides on a single server and for replicating data to multiple servers for redundancy. A comprehensive solution must allow for multiple redundant options for ensuring reliability.
- **Scalability** -- A scalable database solution should be able to support a constantly growing base of users, data, and transactions. Ideally it should be possible to support this growth without requiring new hardware. RDBMS options that are designed to maximize scalability have options for technologies such as parallel processing using multi-processor servers, data compression, in-memory processing, and database virtualization.
- **Manageability** -- Organizations do not always factor in the long-term cost of ownership when choosing between RDBMS options. This can lead to unnecessary extra expenditures in the future. Focusing on software licensing models while ignoring long-term staffing expenditures it a potential pitfall. An RDBMS that provides a streamlined installation, automated tuning and error

correction, and intuitive tooling can help keep administrative personnel costs low.

Selecting an application interface

The vast majority of this exam and this guide is about designing the database. The database consists of tables, indexes, constraints, keys, etc. However, with most databases, the people using it will not directly interface with any of that. Rather they will access the database through an interface provided by a database application. The choice of development environment will affect what the users see and how they will interact with the database.

There are a number of different development tools that can be used to create the interface that will be accessible to the users. The choice of development environment is an important one, although I would rate it as less critical than the choice of RDBMS discussed in the previous chapter. It is not simple to change user interfaces, but certainly is it easier to switch from one user interface to another than it is to switch databases.

One of the first decisions is whether to go with a client-based application tool or a web-based tool. A client-based tool is an application executable that is running on the client machine of the user accessing the database. That executable will make a connection to the database and facilitate communication with the database for the user. By contrast, a web-based tool runs within a Web browser. Because a web page is essentially static, there is no continuous connection between the web-based application and the database. This limits the ability of such applications to interact with the database. On the other hand, web based applications require no installation on the client machine and are therefore much easier to maintain. There are a number of questions that must be answered about the environment into which the tool will be introduced before deciding on the interface to be used, including:

- How many application tiers will be used?
- How will upgrades of the application interface be performed?
- Are the application users local to a single site or spread among multiple sites?
- What are the network capabilities of the organization?
- What are the technical skill levels of the users?
- Is there a legacy interface in place that they are familiar with?

Regardless of the interface chosen, there are many potential pitfalls in developing the application. Some of the best practices when developing a user interface include:

- The interface should have a consistent look throughout.
- It should contain good instructions and help imbedded within it.
- There should be an intuitive look and feel.
- The fields should be well labeled and required vs. optional fields should be tagged.
- When exceptions occur, users should see informative error messages.
- The tool should provide confirmation when actions are performed.

2.2 Identify the activities in the conceptual design phase of a database

Introduction to database design

The initial steps in designing a database can be broken out into the following outline:

1. Gather the business requirements
2. Convert the requirements into sentences and identify nouns
3. Organize the nouns and define attributes
4. Define relationships between nouns and apply constraints

While there are only four steps, each of them can be quite involved. Gathering business requirements, for example, is much easier said than done. Business requirements define the intent of the database to be designed. If they are incomplete, or wrong, then whatever gets designed is almost certain to be a failure. Whenever the initial design is not thought through completely, it runs the risk that each part of the database application will be added to incrementally as the program develops. The result tend to be overly complex and awkward to work with. In extreme cases the application may have to be scrapped and the design project started over from scratch.

If the Imaginary Airlines database were a real design project, it might have started life at a meeting with the company's executives explaining the business and their needs for a database. The initial business requirements might have started life from a statement made by one of the executives such as the following:

"*Imaginary Airlines is in the business of passenger travel. We have a number of aircraft based at several different airports around the United States. We must track thousands of flight reservations every month from our customers. In addition, we must keep meticulous track of the maintenance records for each of our aircraft.*"

Given a set of business requirements like the above, the next step would be to pull out the sentences that are relevant to the database. You should pay particular attention to the nouns and verbs applicable to database design. Initially, look for the nouns in the requirements statement. Nouns will be mapped to entities, which will eventually become tables in the physical database design. From the statement above, there are three sentences that can be created. This results in five unique nouns (in capital letters).

- AIRCRAFT are based at AIRPORTS.
- Track RESERVATIONS from CUSTOMERS.
- Track MAINTENANCE RECORDS for AIRCRAFT

Do not make the mistake of assuming that it will be possible to derive all of the tables needed for a given database from the business requirements alone. It is virtually certain that you will discover a need for additional entities at later stages of the design process. This step will simply provide a starting point.

Once you have developed a set of entities from the nouns, it is necessary to determine what attributes (columns) will be stored in them. During this process, you may determine that one noun from the business requirements will require two tables (or three or four) in the database and so the entity must be split into pieces. Conversely, you might find that two nouns identified during the business requirements might have nearly identical attributes and that only a single table is needed to store the data for both. In this case, the attributes of the two would be combined into a single entity. Making these determinations at this stage of the design process requires much less work than having to retrofit the database once tables have been created and coding has begin.

After the attributes have been determined, the next step is to define the relationships between entities. Relationships can often be determined by using the verbs from the sentences created in step two. For example: "Aircraft are BASED at airports." This implies that individual aircraft in Imaginary Airlines' fleet have one airport that they are primarily associated with. From the verb, we can determine that there is a relationship between the AIRCRAFT and AIRPORTS entities.

Later chapters will go into more details about attributes and relationships, but these steps encapsulate the heart of the design process. As a database developer, you must take the real-world data provided to you by people who know little about databases and construct a set of tables and relationships that maps closely to that data.

Identifying business rules

Capturing business rules during the design phases is very important to database developers because they provide insight into the needs, processes, and required functionality of the database application. A structural business rule indicates the types of information to be stored and how the information elements interrelate. Structural business rules help to define the business information model. As a general rule, structural business rules can be represented in entity relationship models. If you were developing a database application for the purchasing group of an organization, they might tell you something like the following:

"*If a need to buy an item occurs, employees will create a purchase request. One or more purchase orders will be created to serve the purchase request and the purchase order number(s) will be supplied to the vendor providing the item being purchased Vendors will supply the requested item(s) and send one or more invoices against the purchase order.*"

From that statement, we can derive three entities (Purchase Request, Purchase Order, and Invoice) as well as the relationships between the entities. A conceptual model based on that statement might look like the following:

The entity relationship diagram makes it clear that a purchase request may have one or more purchase orders, which in turn may have one or more invoices associated with them.

In contrast to structural business rules, procedural business rules (are also known as process business rules) quite often cannot be represented in an entity relationship diagram. Procedural business rules are often required to ensure that business processes comply with company policies or legal requirements.

One example of a procedural business rule might be a limit on an order system. Customers ordering products from the system might have a credit limit. Once that credit limit has been exceeded, the order system will not allow new orders from the customer in question. Alternately, the system might allow orders so long as the customer has not been marked for a late payment. In either case, logic within the database application must kick in to prevent an otherwise allowable action from occurring due to the business rule.

Rules such as this can often be enforced through the use of database triggers. When a database application attempts to create a new order, an INSERT trigger fires. The trigger checks for the disallowed conditions (i.e. a late payment for the current customer). If a disallowed condition is present, the trigger prevents the insert from occurring. Such a trigger might be implemented at the table level, but more likely would be implemented at the application level to provide the best responsiveness. Since rules like this cannot be displayed on the ERD, they are generally included in the design plan on a separate document.

Some business rules are more complex than simply allowing or disallowing a given action. Often it is necessary for an application to adhere to workflow rules. A workflow rule might indicate that event A must happen before event B, and that events C and D must happen concurrently.

An example of a procedural business rule that requires workflow logic might be an approval process that must be followed when an employee submits a request to take a business trip. An example travel approval workflow might work as follows:

1. An employee must create and submit a travel itinerary for approval.
2. Their immediate manager must approve the travel.
3. The Travel team must validate that all required information has been provided on the itinerary.
4. The Finance team must verify that the funding exists to pay for the trip and that the charge information is correct.
5. A senior manager must approve the travel.
6. The Travel team receives the approved itinerary and books the trip.

Generally in a workflow like the above, programming logic must be created in order to ensure the proper flow of the process. Among other things, it is generally necessary to ensure that only the person in charge of the currently active step can make changes. It would not be acceptable, for example, for the original employee to make changes to the itinerary while it is in step five of the above workflow. This will normally require code in a procedural language such as PL/SQL or Java in order to implement the required logic.

Effects of poor database design practices

It is essentially impossible to create a functional database application for a set of users without understanding their fundamental problems and goals. Before a single snippet of code is written or a table created, the design process must start with an examination of requirements. Capturing requirements is not simply the process of writing down what the users want in a database application. The business requirements have to be met in a fashion that is compatible with the proper functioning of a database.

In 1994 over 350 companies were surveyed by the Standish Group about their software projects. From a pool of over 8000 projects, thirty-one percent were canceled before they were completed. To understand the results better, the following year Standish asked the survey respondents to explain the root causes of the failed projects. The top eight factors were:

1. Incomplete requirements (13.1%)
2. Lack of user involvement (12.4%)
3. Lack of resources (10.6%)
4. Unrealistic expectations (9.9%)
5. Lack of executive support (9.3%)
6. Changing requirements and specifications (8.7%)
7. Lack of planning (8.1%)
8. System no longer needed (7.5%)

Most of the factors supplied involve some aspect of the requirements gathering process. If a concerted effort is not made to understand, document, and manage requirements during the development process, it can lead to a number of problems. There is absolutely no point in building a system that solves the wrong problem, does not function as expected, or is too complex for users to understand or utilize.

Three of the myriad problems and anomalies that are the result of poor database design practices include:

- **Duplicate data** – This is normally caused by incomplete or incorrect normalization practices. Redundant data not only adds unnecessary storage costs to the database, but it can also lead to discrepancies when a single data point stored in two different locations has a different value in each. At this point it becomes difficult to determine which data point is correct. Even if there is code in place to ensure the value is always the same in both locations, that code is a failure point and represents unnecessary complexity in the database application.
- **Poorly mapped data** – It is unfortunately common for developers to map incoming data to the wrong data types. Mapping date/time data to character fields is one of the most common. All relational databases have fields specifically designed to handle date information. Using these fields prevents the entry of invalid information (e.g. February 31st) and allows the use of any date functions built into the RDBMS Against the stored data. When the

wrong data types are used, the result is generally that the utility of the stored data is significantly diminished.
- **Loss of data integrity** – When two or more tables are related, changes to data in one table should take into account related data in other tables. For example, a given aircraft in the Imaginary Airlines AIRCRAFT_FLEET table has ten flights associated with it in the AIRCRAFT_FLIGHTS table. In turn, those flights have multiple customer reservations stored in the FLIGHT_RESERVATIONS table. In a database with poorly-designed constraints (or no constraints), it might be possible to delete the record for that aircraft. The result would either be that all of the related flights and associated reservations would be deleted as well, or that they remain in the database... but have no associated aircraft. In either case, potentially hundreds of airline customers would be affected.
- **Inflexibility** – Users tend to provide information about what normally happens. All too often this means that databases are designed without any thought to exceptions in the data. Database designs that have no means for handling data exceptions that are unusual (but legitimate for the business model) will cause development headaches once they go to production.

The above are not intended to be a comprehensive list of potential problems by any means. There are dozens of ways in which a poorly designed database can cause failures. It is incumbent on database developers to make every effort to create a comprehensive design before starting development of a new database application.

Database design phases

The below diagram was introduced in section 1.3, but it is worth revisiting again here. The three database design phases are Conceptual, Logical, and Physical. The conceptual model starts off with a very high-level, low-detail view of the data to be stored. At the Logical and Physical phases, additional information is added to the model to bring the design close to what must be created in order to have a working database system.

Feature	Conceptual	Logical	Physical
Entity Names	✓	✓	
Entity Relationships	✓	✓	
Attributes		✓	
Primary Keys		✓	✓
Foreign Keys		✓	✓
Table Names			✓
Column Names			✓
Column Data Types			✓

The conceptual phase is intended only to create a data model for the organization. The intended audience is primarily business users. Providing a significant level of detail to these users is likely to be counterproductive. As a result, the conceptual ERD simply displays the primary entities that will be storing the data needed by the organization. This will allow them to more easily confirm that the design appears to correctly model the flow of data.

The logical phase adds details about the attributes to be stored and provides specifics on the relationship between entities. It is also at this stage that data normalization is performed. Normalizing the data means that the entities displayed in the Logical model may not precisely map to the conceptual model.

During the physical phase, it is necessary to take into account the specific database that will be used by the database being created. The DBMS system determines the specific data types that will be used to store the attributes identified during the logical model phase. The result of the physical design phase will be used directly to generate the DDL statements that create the tables, constraints, and foreign key relationships that will make up the database.

Conceptual database design

This design phase is used when the database developer is working with the organization and/or users that will be using the database application being created. At the concept stage, you are constructing an extremely high-level view of the various data elements that need to be stored and how they inter-relate. A conceptual data model is normally created at an early stage in the design process of a new application. It is primarily a business model viewed from a data perspective. Conceptual data models are designed primarily for a business audience rather than a technical one. Once created, the model should be reviewed by the business to locate any missing elements.

Conceptual data models do not act as a solution model and are both application and technology neutral. They generally take the form of an entity relationship diagram (ERD) and identify the highest-level relationships between the different entities. They are developed in order to understand and capture business knowledge from the perspective of data flows.

A well-designed conceptual data model should include all of the key business entities for which the organization wants to collect data as well as the relationships between them. As a general rule attributes are not included in conceptual data models.

Depending on the specific ER style used, the conceptual model can look a bit different. The same ER diagram as the above created using the Chen model would looks something like the below:

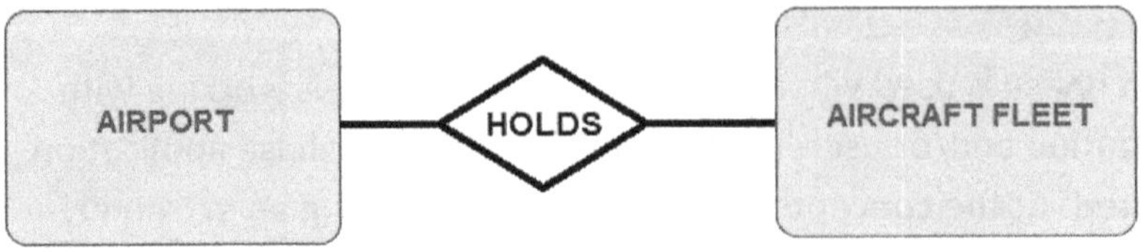

As has been noted, typically in the conceptual diagram, none of the entities will have attributes listed. However, I have *occasionally* seen some conceptual models where attributes are listed – but broken out from their entity as in the below diagram:

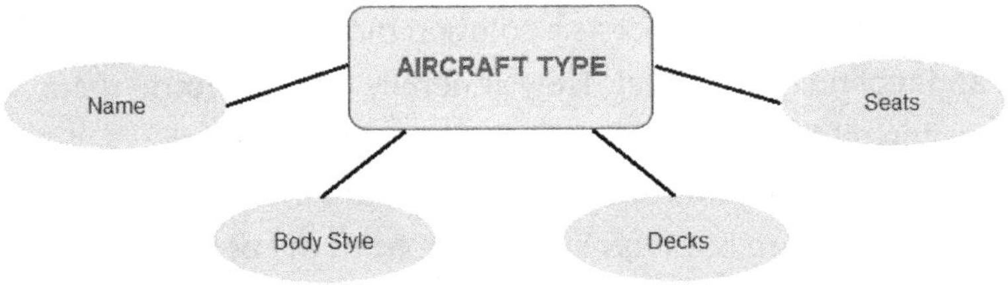

The ovals are used only in the Chen ER model. Specifically, the three ER shapes used to denote entities, attributes and relationship in the Chen model are:

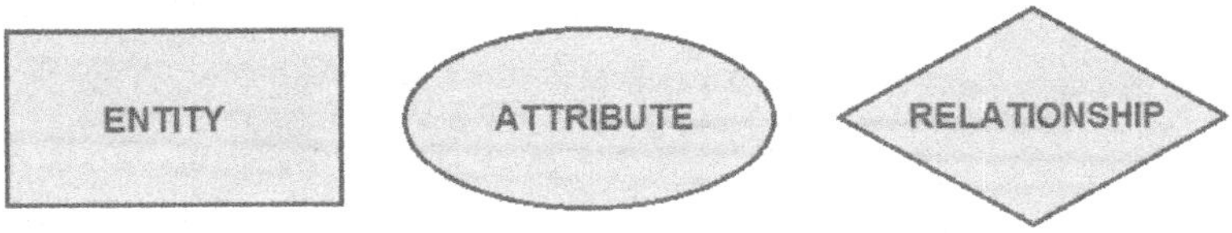

Entity-Relationship (ER) models

Entity-relationship models (normally abbreviated as ER models) provide a means for graphically representing the logical relationships of entities when designing a database. Peter Pin-Shan Chen of Massachusetts

Institute of Technology (MIT) is credited with being the first to suggest the use of ER modeling when he published a paper about Entity-Relationship modeling in 1976. Today there are a number of different styles of ER models in use. When a diagram is created of a database using the ER-model, the result is called an Entity-Relationship Diagram or ERD.

The entity–relationship model is used to provide a means of visualizing a given area of business data rather than defining business processes. The data to be captured in the database is represented as entities. Entities can be thought of as nouns. For example an airplane, a customer, or a flight reservation would all be candidates for an entity. Entities are connected to each other by relationships. Relationships between entities express the dependencies and requirements between them. Relationships can be thought of as verbs linking two or more nouns. For example, a customer purchases a flight reservation or an airplane is based at an airport. Entities can have attributes associated with them that further characterize the data being stored. For example, an entity called CUSTOMER would logically have attributes such as: first name, last name, home address, and email.

ER models can be created at three broad levels:

- **Conceptual data model** -- The conceptual model contains the least granular detail of the three. It is used to describe a database at an extremely high level and establish the scope of what will be included within the model. A conceptual model is generally created as the foundation for one or more logical data models.
- **Logical data model** - A logical ER model may be created from a conceptual model or it may be the starting point when designing a new database. A logical model ER contains additional details beyond what is contained in a conceptual model ER. The attributes of data entity are added and the relationships between entities are established with more precision.
- **Physical data model** -- Physical model ERs contain additional information beyond that shown in a logical model ER. Creating a physical model ER is normally one of the last steps prior to developed creating a database. The physical model ER should contain sufficient details to produce the database. Physical model

ERs are specific to the RDBMS for which they are designed to be created in.

The below diagram provides examples of several different ER diagram conventions:

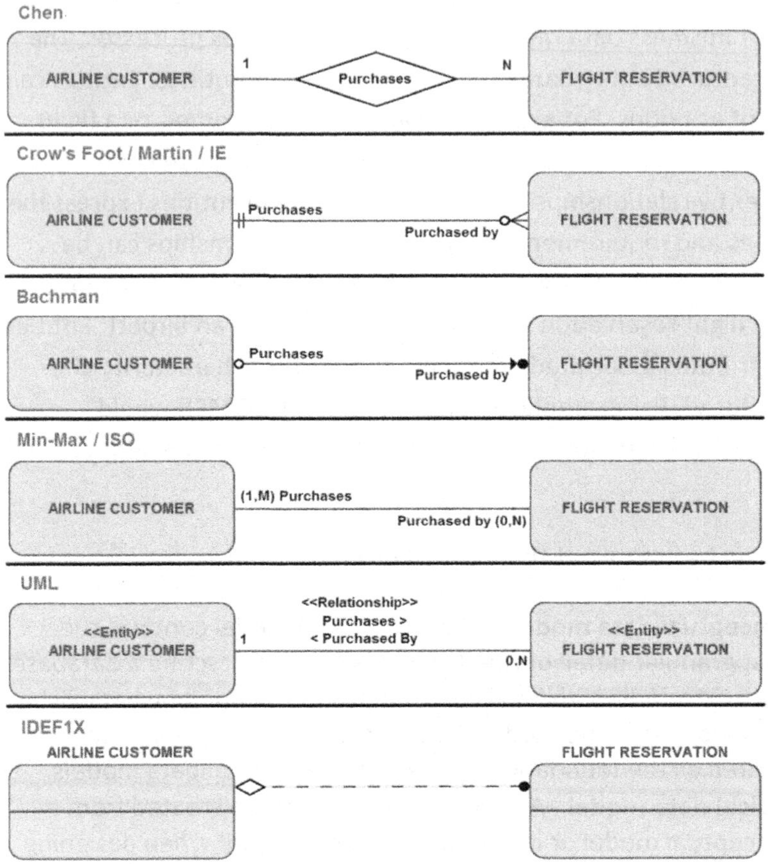

Domain 3: Normalization and Database Design

3.1 Apply normalization techniques and processes

What is normalization?

One of the more significant goals in a well-designed relational database is for the data stored to be properly normalized. The primary purpose of normalization is to eliminate redundancy in a database. Ideally, each unique piece of data should be stored in only a single location. The major benefit of normalization is that this makes it easy to maintain the data. If a change must be made, it only needs to be made in a single location. A secondary benefit of normalization comes from space savings, but that is eclipsed by the ease of maintenance. Normalization is part of successful relational database design. When a relational database has not been properly normalized, the resulting application may be inaccurate, slow, and inefficient. When normalizing a database, there are four goals:

- Arranging data into logical groupings such that each describes a small part of the whole
- Minimizing the amount of duplicate data stored in the database
- Organizing the data such that data changes need to occur in only a single location.
- Designing a table structure that allows data to be accessed and manipulated quickly and efficiently while retaining data integrity.

One of the acknowledged downsides of normalization is that it increases the number of tables in the database. As a consequence, more joins are required when querying data. In extreme cases, this can lead to slower database performance. For this reason, it is not unheard of to de-normalize data in some instances. De-normalizing data is not a step that is performed without careful consideration. The benefits of a fully normalized database are significant, so this is a step that is generally only performed when it has been determined <u>both</u> that normalization has caused a performance problem and that de-normalization resolves the issue.

Normal forms

The term 'normalization' was first used with databases by E.F.Codd, the creator of the relational model. It refers to the process of organizing the logical structure of a database in order to facilitate both ad-hoc queries and data updates. The most common term you will encounter as a database developer when dealing with normalization is 'Third Normal Form', sometimes abbreviated as 3NF. A table is in third normal form when it meets all of the following three rules:

- **First rule of normalization** -- A table shall contain no repeating groups.
- **Second rule of normalization** -- If a table has a compound primary key, and one or more fields in a table depend on only part of the primary key for that table, move them to a separate table along with that part of the key.
- **Third rule of normalization** -- If one or more fields in a table do not depend at all on the primary key for that table (or any part of it), move them to a separate table along with copies of the fields on which they do depend.

A fourth normal form is known as Boyce-Codd normalization (BCNF). The definition for this form is that a relation R(X) is in Boyce–Codd Normal Form if for every non-trivial functional dependency Y → Z defined on it, Y contains a key K of R(X). That is, Y is a superkey for R(X).

Determinants and dependencies

To be able to normalize entities, it is necessary to understand determinants and dependants. A determinant is any attribute (simple or composite) on which some other attribute is fully functionally dependent. The terms determinant and dependent can be described as follows:

- The expression **A → B** means 'if I know the value of A, then I can obtain the value of B.'
- In the expression **A → B**, A is the determinant and B is the dependent attribute.
- The value A determines the value of B.
- The value B depends on the value of A.

When more than one attribute acts as the determinant for an entity, it is possible for the dependent attributes to be fully or partially dependent. Given an entity for four attributes, A, B, C and D, where **AB → CD**:

- **Fully Functional Dependency** -- The entity has a fully functional dependency if both A & B are required in order to know the values of both C & D. That is to say, **AB → CD**, and **A does not→ CD** and **B does not→ CD.**
- **Partially Functional Dependency** -- The entity has a partially functional dependency if both A & B are **not** required in order to know the values of both C & D. That is to say, **AB → CD**, and any of the following are also true: **A → C** or **A → D** or **B → C** or **B → D**.

First normal form

In order for an entity (or database table) to satisfy the requirements for first normal form, several things must be true:

- The entity must have a primary key and that primary key must have a unique value for all rows/tuples. At least one attribute in each tuple must be unique (that one attribute might be the primary key).
- Attribute values must be atomic and not decomposable.
- There must be no repeating groups of attributes.
- All attributes must depend on the primary key.

In the conceptual stage of documenting the Imaginary Airlines tables, an AIRCRAFT_FLEET entity was proposed. When converting to the logical model, it was determined that the following information about IA's fleet of aircraft needed to be stored in that entity:

HOME_AIRPORT	APT_ABBR	TYPE	BODY_STYLE	DECKS	SEATS	TAIL_NUM
Atlanta, GA	ATL	Boeing 737	Narrow	Single	200	IA374GL2
Atlanta, GA	ATL	Boeing 757	Narrow	Single	240	IA47GHE3
Dallas/Fort Worth	DFW	Boeing 747	Wide	Double	416	IA47KJE4
Dallas/Fort Worth	DFW	Boeing 767	Wide	Single	350	IA47SDW5
Miami, FL	MIA	Boeing 747	Wide	Double	416	IA47KJS6,IA47LEY7
Orlando, FL	MCO	Boeing 767	Wide	Single	350	IA67AWY8,IA67AQOE9

Given the above set of attributes and data, this entity fails the test for first normal form for a number of reasons.

1. The TAIL_NUM attribute is not atomic. The bottom two lines in the example above have information in them that is decomposable – namely two separate aircraft tail numbers.
2. There are repeating groups of attributes. The HOME_AIRPORT and APT_ABBR from one set and the TYPE, BODY_STYLE, DECKS, and SEATS another set of repeating attributes.
3. No attribute is suitable for a primary key.

To fix problem number one, the non-atomic attributes must be broken out into separate tuples, as per the below diagram:

HOME_AIRPORT	APT_ABBR	TYPE	BODY_STYLE	DECKS	SEATS	TAIL_NUM
Atlanta, GA	ATL	Boeing 737	Narrow	Single	200	IA374GL2
Atlanta, GA	ATL	Boeing 757	Narrow	Single	240	IA47GHE3
Dallas/Fort Worth	DFW	Boeing 747	Wide	Double	416	IA47KJE4
Dallas/Fort Worth	DFW	Boeing 767	Wide	Single	350	IA47SDW5
Miami, FL	MIA	Boeing 747	Wide	Double	416	IA47KJS6
Miami, FL	MIA	Boeing 747	Wide	Double	416	IA47LEY7
Orlando, FL	MCO	Boeing 767	Wide	Single	350	IA67AQOE9
Orlando, FL	MCO	Boeing 767	Wide	Single	350	IA67AWY8

Solving the second problem requires breaking out the repeating groups to separate entities. Moving the attributes with repeating groups out yields the two new entities below:

HOME_AIRPORT	APT_ABBR
Atlanta, GA	ATL
Dallas/Fort Worth	DFW
Miami, FL	MIA
Orlando, FL	MCO

TYPE	BODY_STYLE	DECKS	SEATS
Boeing 737	Narrow	Single	200
Boeing 757	Narrow	Single	240
Boeing 747	Wide	Double	416
Boeing 767	Wide	Single	350

The only reasonable candidate key values that exist in the two new entities are APT_ABBR and TYPE respectively. Removing all but these keys from the original entity yields the following result:

APT_ABBR	TYPE	TAIL_NUM
ATL	Boeing 737	IA374GL2
ATL	Boeing 757	IA47GHE3
DFW	Boeing 747	IA47KJE4
DFW	Boeing 767	IA47SDW5
MIA	Boeing 747	IA47KJS6
MIA	Boeing 747	IA47LEY7
MCO	Boeing 767	IA67AQOE9
MCO	Boeing 767	IA67AWY8

At this point, the three entities meet all of the requirements of first normal form.

Second normal form

In order for a table to be compliant with second-normal form, it must already be first-normal form compliant. The second normal form rule deals with entities that have a primary key composed of multiple columns. Any entity in 1NF with a single column key is automatically second-normal form compliant. However, when multiple key columns exist, all non-key attributes must depend on the whole key and not just a portion of it. There can be no partially functional dependencies.

The FLIGHT_RESERVATIONS entity is shown below. The flight ID (FLT_ID) and customer ID (CST_ID) columns make up the primary key.

FLT_ID	CST_ID	RSV_DATE	RSV_STATUS	BASE_AIRFARE	DISCOUNT	GOLD_CUST
276	1286	2-Jul-14	Paid	120	0	N
289	1731	13-Sep-14	Paid	120	0	N
307	275	1-Sep-14	Paid	120	10	Y
328	2516	2-Jul-14	Paid	120	0	N
435	740	28-Jun-14	Paid	120	30	Y
578	156	5-Jul-14	Paid	120	0	N
633	387	2-Jul-14	Paid	120	0	N

Because this entity has a compound primary key, it must be checked for second-normal form compliance. The Reservation Date, Reservation Status, Base Airfare, and Discount all apply to the specific reservation made for the given flight ID booked by the customer. They depends on both keys. However, the Gold Customer flag depends on the customer ID key alone. Removing this attribute from the entity will make it second-normal form compliant.

Third normal form

In order for a relation to be in third normal form, it must be in second normal form and it must have no transitive dependencies. A transitive dependency can only occur if a relation has three or more attributes. Consider A, B, and C as three distinct attributes in the relation (or distinct groups of attributes). Suppose the following three statements are true:

1. For a given value of A, the value of B is known (**A → B**)
2. It is not true that given the value of B that the value of A is known. (**B does not → A**)
3. For a given value of B, the value of C is known (**B → C**)

Given **A → B** and **B → C**, there is a functional dependency **A → C** due to the axiom of transitivity (which is why this is called a transitive dependency). The relation below contains a transitive dependency:

AIRCRAFT_MODEL	SEATS	MANUFACTURER	MANUFACTURER_HQ
Boeing 747	416	Boeing	Chicago, IL
Boeing 767	350	Boeing	Chicago, IL
Boeing 737	200	Boeing	Chicago, IL
Boeing 757	240	Boeing	Chicago, IL
Airbus A320	200	Airbus	Blagnac, France
Airbus A380	525	Airbus	Blagnac, France
Lockheed L-1011	350	Lockheed	Bethesda, MD

The functional dependency {Aircraft Model} → {Manufacture HQ} is true. That is, if we know the model of aircraft, it follows that the location of the manufacturer's headquarters is also known. The following three statements are also true:

- {Aircraft Model} → {Manufacturer}
- {Manufacturer} does not → {Aircraft Model}
- {Manufacturer} → {Manufacturer HQ}

Therefore {Aircraft Model} → {Manufacturer HQ} is a transitive dependency. The transitive dependency occurs because a non-key attribute (Manufacturer) is determining another non-key attribute (Manufacturer HQ). To resolve the dependency, the Manufacturer HQ attribute must be pulled out to a separate entity.

Boyce-Codd normal form (BCNF)

BCNF is a slightly stronger version of the third normal form. I have never met anyone outside academics that referenced or cared about BCNF. If it were not in the test, I would have left it out of this guide completely.

BCNF deals with redundancy in the primary key. It is rare for a table that meets the requirements for 3NF to not meet the requirements of BCNF as well. If the 3NF table does not have multiple overlapping candidate keys, then a table in 3NF will always be in BCNF. A table that is in 3NF with two or more overlapping candidate keys may or may not meet the requirements for BCNF depending on its functional dependencies.

BCNF is tied to the concept of a determinant. As noted earlier, a determinant is any attribute (simple or composite) on which some other attribute is fully functionally dependent. An entity is in Boyce-Code Normal Form if and only if every determinant is a candidate key.

The only time I have ever seen BCNF make any sense is one case where someone had made an example table that did not comply with it. However, that example table required ridiculously contrived logic for why the fields had the relationships that they did. I tried to create an example table to use here. Unfortunately I kept banging my head against an excess of common sense. I failed miserably in coming up with a table that was a good example for something that passed 3NF but failed BCNF. If you really want to punish yourself with this useless bit of information, I suggest Googling for "BCNF example". My suggestion would be to use the rule I stated earlier: **If the 3NF table does not have multiple overlapping candidate keys, then a table in 3NF will always be in BCNF**. Therefore, if a table is not in 3NF, you don't have to worry about BCNF. If a table is in 3NF and only has one possible primary key, you do not have to worry about BCNF. It is only when a table is in 3NF and there are multiple attributes or groups of attributes that are candidates to be a primary key that the possibility of the table being in 3NF but not BCNF becomes an issue.

3.2 Describe logical database design steps and practices

Logical database design

One step beyond the conceptual stage is the logical database design process. That said – in the real world it is often where my database design process starts. I will often skip the conceptual design stage when I have sufficient knowledge of the organization. The conceptual design model is primarily intended to facilitate working with stakeholders of the database application being built. The logical database design process, by contrast, is where the real work in laying out the elements required to build the database begins. Some of the many steps that are performed during the logical design phase include:

- Add attributes to entities
- Identify and remove redundant attributes
- Begin normalization of the entities
- Identify relationships between entities
- Resolve many to many (M:N) relationships
- Identify and resolve complex relationships
- Identify and resolve recursive relationships
- Identify relationships with attributes

One of the most obvious differences between the conceptual and logical data models is that the logical data model includes attributes and breaks out operational and transactional entities. The two diagrams below model the same set of data. The first was created using the conceptual model and the second using the logical model.

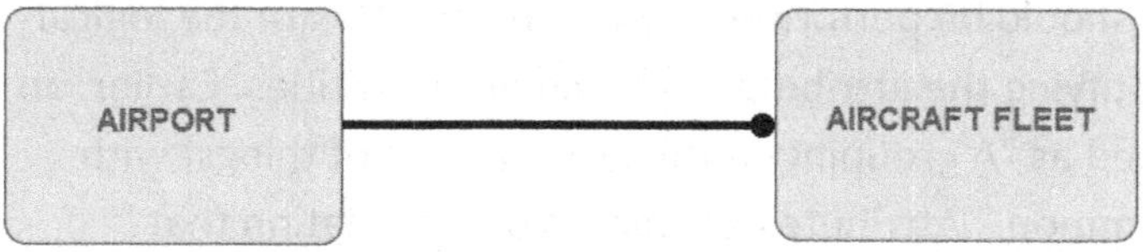

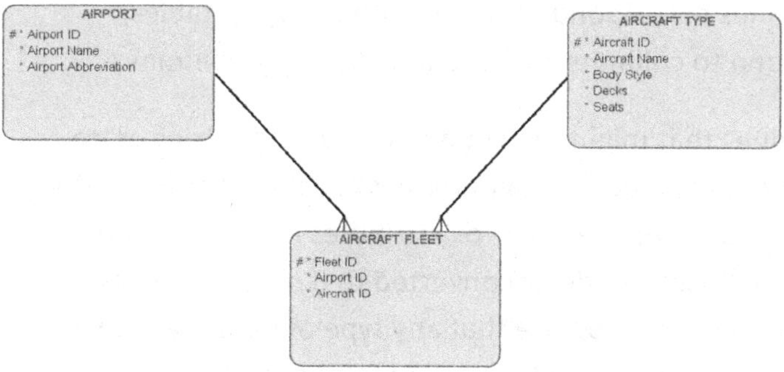

Creating a logical data model

If the database design process started with a conceptual model of the database to be created, creating the logical model is a matter of refining that model and adding details. While the conceptual model generally only contains master data entities, the logical model will contain operational and transactional data entities. One example of this is the "AIRCRAFT TYPE" entity that appears in the logical model but not the conceptual model in the previous section. To the stakeholders of the database, there are a number of planes in Imaginary Airlines' fleet and each is based at an airport. They do not mentally break out the specific type of plane independently from the aircraft itself. The "AIRCRAFT TYPE" entity is broken out from the "AIRCRAFT FLEET" entity as part of the normalization that occurs while creating the logical data model. Ideally when completed, the logical data model should be compliant with third-normal form. In reality, it is likely that normalization will not be completed until some point during the physical design.

Attributes

Another step that should be performed during the creation of the logical data model is identifying the attributes for each of the entities. Earlier, an entity was described as "A grouping of things (or a class of things) with rules or data in common." Attributes are pieces of information that provide information about a property or characteristic of that entity. They might describe or quantify or qualify some aspect of the entity. In the same way that entities correspond to tables without being tables, attributes correspond to columns without actually being columns.

Attributes have values that might be a number, character string, date, image, or any other information the database is capable of storing. The specific class of data is never specified for attributes and will not be determined until the logical model is converted to a physical model. However, it is important to recognize that any type of data that can be used to describe the entity is a valid candidate for an attribute.

In the below diagram there are five entities shown along with a set of attributes that might be used for them.

Entity	Attributes
Airport	Name, Code, Location
Aircraft Type	Name, Body style, Decks, Seats
Flight	Departure Point, Destination, Date
Ticket	Flight #, Cost, Seat, Date
Passenger	Name, Flight Count, Gold Club, Last Flight

The volatility of an attribute is determined by how often the value changes. If the data in a given attribute changes often, it is considered volatile. If the information seldom changes, it is considered non-volatile. Sometimes the volatility of a piece of data depends on how it is stored in the database.

For example, Imaginary Airlines periodically has ticket price specials that last sixty days. When a new discount program is added to their "Fare Special" entity, the time limit could be provided by a numeric attribute that held a value of the number of days until the sale ended. Alternately, the entity could use a date attribute that stored the last day of the special fares. The 'days until end' option would result in an extremely volatile attribute that would have to decrement by one every 24 hours. The 'end date' attribute would be very non-volatile since the value would never have to change. Whenever there is an option between choosing a volatile over a non-volatile attribute, generally it is better to pick the non-volatile attribute.

Relationships

One of the most important parts of the logical design process is clarifying the relationships between entities. Relationships denote the way in which two entities interconnect. One or more attributes for an entity connect to an equivalent number of attributes in (normally) a second entity. It is also possible for a single entity to have a relationship between two or more attributes within itself. There are several rules when creating relationships:

- A relationship can exist between a maximum of two entities.
- A relationship can exist on the same entity.
- A relationship has two perspectives.
- Both perspectives of a relationship can be labeled.

One of the aspects of a relationship is optionality. There are two possible values:

- **Mandatory Relationship** -- A mandatory relationship specifies that each instance from an entity must be related to another instance. This is represented by a straight line.
- **Optional Relationship** -- An optional relationship specifies that each instance from an entity may be related to another instance. This is represented by a dashed line.

Perspectives indicate how a given relationship can be described from the viewpoint of each end. Every relationship will have two perspectives. The perspective is determined by the optionality and cardinality/ordinality of the relationship.

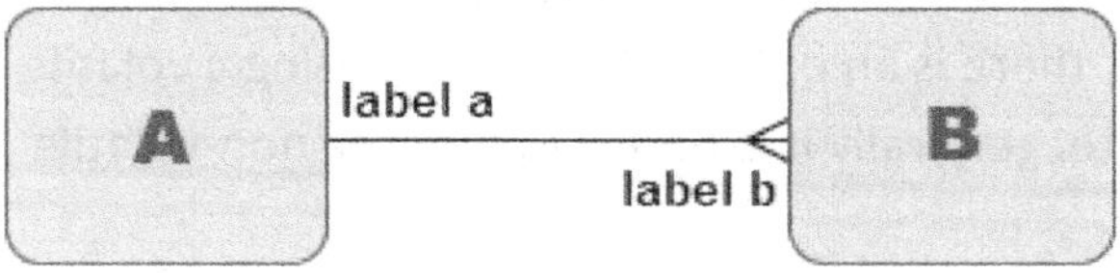

Using the diagram above, the two perspectives would be:

- **First Perspective / A Perspective** -- Each 'A' must 'label a' one or more Bs
- **Second Perspective / B Perspective** -- Each 'B' must 'label b' exactly one A.

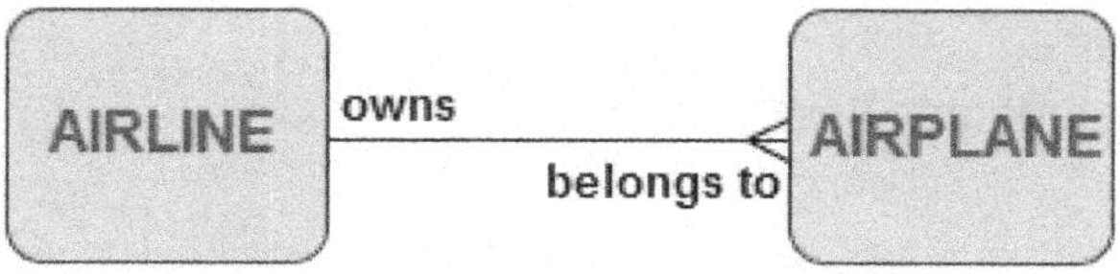

If the entities in question were called Airline and Airplane respectively, the perspectives could be stated as follows:

- **First Perspective / Airline Perspective** -- Each Airline must own one or more Airplanes.
- **Second Perspective / Airplane Perspective** -- Each Airplane must belong to exactly one Airline.

When the relationship is optional, the perspectives would be:

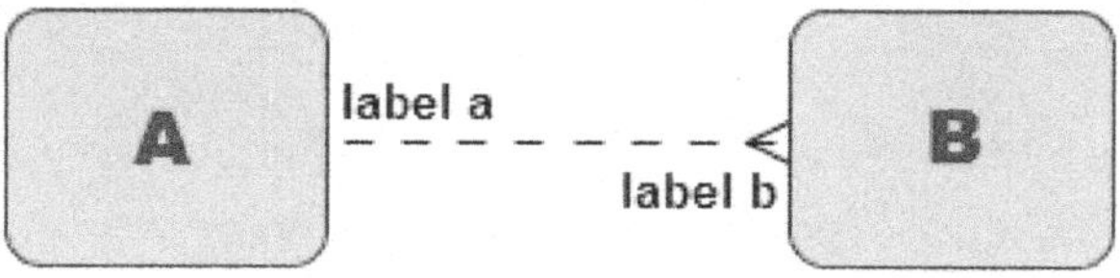

- **First Perspective / A Perspective** -- Each 'A' may 'label a' one or more Bs
- **Second Perspective / B Perspective** -- Each 'B' may 'label b' exactly one A.

Speaking in ERDish

Both perspectives of a relationship can be described using ERDish. This is a means of accurately expressing the relationships between entities in an ERD. Essentially it is a structured process for creating sentences to describe a relationship. When constructing a sentence in ERDish, there are six components:

1. EACH
2. Entity A
3. OPTIONALITY (must be/may be)

4. RELATIONSHIP NAME
5. CARDINALITY (one and only one/ one or more)
6. Entity B

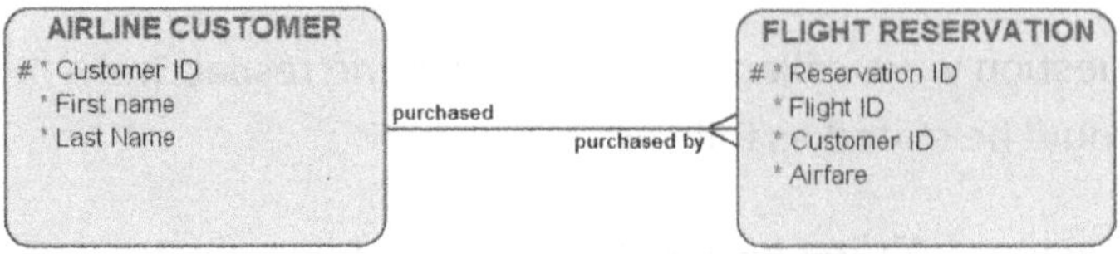

Returning to the diagram with the Airline Customer and Flight Reservation entities (above), the ERDish sentence from left to right would be:

1. EACH
2. Airline Customer
3. must have
4. purchased
5. one or more
6. Flight Reservations

Reading from right to left, the ERDish sentence would be:

1. EACH
2. Flight Reservation
3. must have been
4. purchased by
5. one
6. Airline Customer

It is also possible to reverse the process by using an ERDich sentence to derive the corresponding ERD. As an example, the following two ERDish sentences could be used to develop an ERD.

1. EACH
2. Library
3. will
4. contain
5. one or more
6. Books

1. EACH
2. Book
3. might be
4. contained in
5. one
6. Library

Hopefully it is obvious that the two entities involved are Library and Book. Based on the value in the third bullet of each ERDish sentence, it is possible to determine that the relationship is mandatory on the left and optional on the right. The fifth bullet point on the first ERDish sentence tells us that this is a one-to-many relationship between Library and Book. The ERD would therefore look like the following:

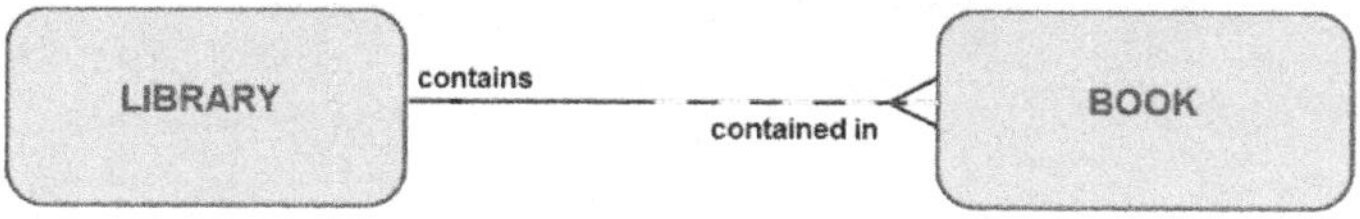

Resolving many-to-many relationships

There is no direct method in the relational model that supports a many-to-many relationship between two entities. In the relational model, a child entity inherits the primary key of a parent entity. In many-to-many relationships, neither of the two entities can be considered the parent or the child. In order to make the situation map to the relational model, a third construct is required to resolve the relationship. For this reason, intersection entities are sometimes referred to as "resolving entities". For that matter, they are sometimes known as associative entities.

An intersection entity is located 'between' the first two and has a one-to-many relationship with each of them. It can be thought of as both an entity and a relationship since it has properties of both. An intersection entity must contain the primary keys from both of the original entities. It may or may not also contain its own unique identifier and possibly additional attributes beyond the keys from the base entities. In the diagram below, the Airline Customer entity has a many-to-many relationship with the Aircraft Flight entity. A given customer may book several different flights with Imaginary Airlines. Likewise, a given flight will have many passengers. The Flight Reservation entity acts as the intersection entity in this relationship. It has the unique identifiers from both the Airline Customer and Aircraft Flight entities, but also a unique identifier of its own. It can also store additional information specific to the intersection such as the airfare, reservation date, discount, etc.

Barred relationships

The unique identifier (UID) of an intersection entity sometimes consists of the primary keys from the originating relationships. When this is true, the relationships will create a composite UID with a barred relationship to the two entities with the many-to-many relationship. In some references, you will see this indicated as the 'preferred' method for creating the UID of an intersection entity. In the diagram below, the unique identifier for the Aircraft Fleet entity is made up of the primary key for the Airports and Aircraft Types entities. This is a barred relationship and is represented by the bar next to the crow's foot of the two relationships.

Personally, I detest doing that and would never do so in an application that I have control over. The instances created by an intersection entity are often referenced by additional entities. In my experience, intersection entities generally have an existence beyond simply relating the original two entities. For example, each instance of the aircraft fleet represents a physical aircraft in the Imaginary Airlines fleet. Other entities in the ERD may well need to reference aircraft in that table. Ideally they should be able to do so with an identifier that is specific to a given plane rather than being a composite UID from two other entities.

In the image below, the Flight Reservation has a UID specific to it. This is the model that I would recommend. Just as with an instance of the Aircraft Fleet, an instance of the Flight Reservation entity has a reason for existence beyond linking Airline Customers with Aircraft Flights. It makes sense for the entity to have its own key to use in relationships. It is also worth noting that in a real world application, the table corresponding to the Aircraft Flight entity would almost certainly have a column that represented the specific plane used for the flight (i.e. the UID of the Aircraft Fleet entity).

Unique identifiers

Any attributes assigned to an entity must be one of three types:

- **Unique Identifier** -- A UID is an attribute whose value uniquely identifies an entity instance. These attributes will be marked with a pound '#' symbol.
- **Mandatory Attribute** - A mandatory attribute is one whose value cannot be null. These attributes will be marked with an asterisk '*' symbol.

- **Optional Attribute** -- An optional attribute is one whose value can be null. These attributes will be marked with a lower-case ‘o’.

When the attributes of an entity have their types properly assigned, identifying the attribute which will become the primary key in the associated table is straightforward. In the below diagram, the Employee ID field will presumably become the primary key. The reason that I say ‘presumably’ is that many developers (including myself) make it a practice to always use artificial or surrogate keys rather than natural keys that are present in the data. That aside, any questions in the exam should expect you to identify the primary key using the '#' symbol in the ERD.

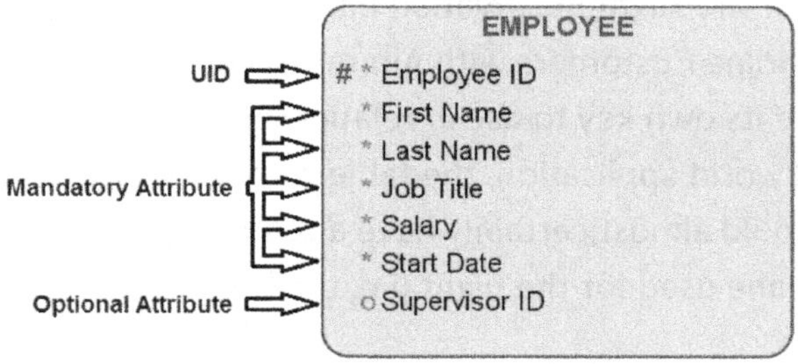

A unique identifier (sometimes abbreviated UID) is a meaningful value that is associated with the data being stored in a table that is never duplicated. It can identify the unique instance by using one or more attributes and/or relationships. Potential unique identifiers depend on the data being stored. Some examples include:

- A table storing employee data might well have a column that contains a personnel number.
- A table of students at a university might have a student ID column.
- A contacts table might have a phone number column.
- An inventory table might have a serial number column.

Regardless, it is possible to use a unique identifier as the primary key column for that table. Once the UID column has been designated as the primary key for a table, the RDBMS will prevent duplicate values from being accidentally (or intentionally) stored in the column.

Primary UIDs

Primary UIDs are identified in an ERD by showing a pound sign (#) to the left of the attribute or attributes that make up the unique identifier. This makes it simple to identify the attributes that will become the primary keys in the physical model.

It is worth noting that foreign keys are not specifically marked in an ERD. The method for identifying the attributes that make up a foreign key is by using the primary UID from the related entity. Foreign key relationships will always use an attribute (or attributes) in the child entity that match the primary UID in the parent entity. The attribute(s) in the child entity will normally have the same name as what exists in the parent. In cases where they do not, unless the ERD was made by someone very bad at their job, the matching attributes should be obvious.

In the diagram below, the Flight Reservation entity is the child of both the Airline Customer and Aircraft Flight entities. The foreign key attribute for the relationship with the Airline Customer entity is 'Customer ID', and the foreign key attribute for the relationship with the Aircraft Flight entity is 'Flight ID'.

There are several different classes of UIDs that can be used in a logical database model:

- **Single Attribute UID** -- A single UID attribute is when an entity is made up of a single UID attribute which is not a foreign key. In the image below, the Airport entity has Airport ID as a single attribute UID.

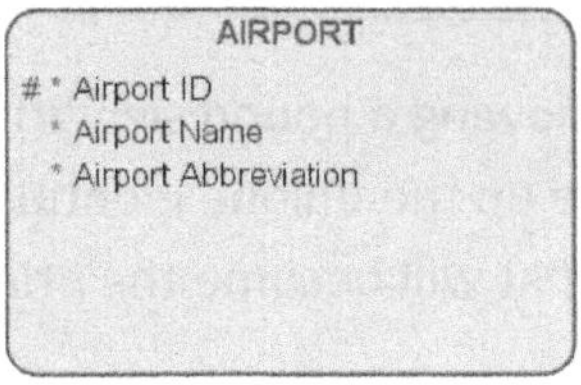

- **Composite Attribute UID** -- A composite UID attribute is when a unique identifier is made up of multiple attributes all of which are not foreign keys. In the image below, the Aircraft Type entity has Aircraft Name and Aircraft Block as a multiple attribute UID.

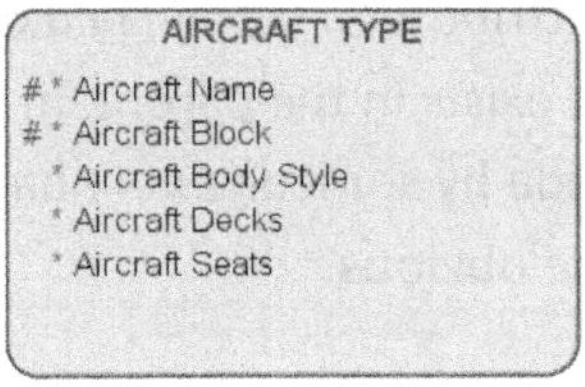

- **Composed Attribute UID** -- A composed UID attribute is when an entity has a primary key which is also a foreign key. In the image below, the Aircraft Fleet entity has a foreign key composed of the primary keys from the Airports and Aircraft Types entities. These are marked with a UID bar by the crow's foot.

- **Composed Cascade Attribute UID** -- A composed cascade UID attribute is when an entity uses its foreign keys as primary keys from an entity with composed UID attributes. In the image below, the Aircraft Flight entity uses the composed attribute UID from the Aircraft Fleet table as part of its primary key – and includes a third attribute, Flight ID, to indicate the specific flight for a given aircraft.

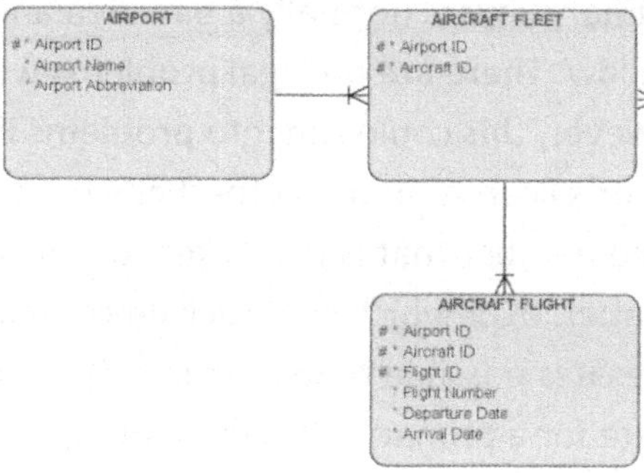

Candidate UIDs

When an entity contains more than one attribute that could identify the row of data uniquely, each of the attributes is considered to be a candidate unique identifier. However, when this happens, only one of the attributes can be selected as the Primary UID. All other attributes would be considered Secondary UIDs. For example, a trucking company might have several candidate UIDs for their drivers, including Social Security Number, Driver's License number, and employee ID. The three UID possibilities then are the following:

- **Candidate UID** – When an entity contains multiple different attributes that could be used to uniquely identify each instance, they are all considered to be candidate UIDs.
- **Primary UID** – An entity can contain multiple candidate UIDs, but only a single primary UID.
- **Secondary UID** – When an entity contains more than one candidate UID, any UIDs that are not selected as the primary UID are considered secondary UIDs.

When multiple attributes can be used as the primary UID, it is generally left up to the organization to determine which one to use. Generally a business would use the UID over which it had the most control. In the trucking company example there are three potential Primary UIDs. Using social security numbers for primary keys is normally a bad idea and in some cases can be against the law. There are no legal problems with using a driver's license number. However, this could run into problems if an employee were to change driver's license numbers (perhaps because they moved to a different state). The number that is least likely to cause problems is the employee number, over which the trucking company has complete control. In most cases it is possible to use similar chains of logic to determine the best candidate for a primary UID when multiple candidates exist.

Artificial unique identifiers

Artificial unique identifiers are values which get created expressly for identification purposes. In the example of the trucking company, all three UIDs: the SSN, driver's license number, and employee number are all artificial UIDs. Many database developers routinely use unique identifiers for primary keys. For example, in the AIRPORTS table below, the three-letter airport code in the APT_ABBR column could have been used as the primary key. This value is supposed to be a globally unique identifier for airports.

AIRPORTS

APT_ID	APT_NAME	APT_ABBR
1	Orlando, FL	MCO
2	Atlanta, GA	ATL
3	Miami, FL	MIA
4	Jacksonville, FL	JAX
5	Dallas/Fort Worth	DFW
7	Houston, TX	IAH

At this point, I feel compelled to exit 'Test Mode' and enter 'Real World Mode'. It is my advice as a developer with a couple of decades writing database applications that you should always use artificial unique identifiers for primary keys. This is also known as a surrogate primary key. Primary keys for tables that I create are always a single column that has an artificially created value (an increasing sequence of numbers). The only downside is that surrogate primary keys have no descriptive value, which is to say that they do not provide any useful information about the table row they identify. There is also a cost in disk space usage, but a negligible one.

Surrogate keys are created only as a tool for the database developer. They have no value for database users and as a general rule should be hidden by the user interface. The reason that I recommend using surrogate keys is that unique identifiers that are not **created** by the database developer are generally not under the **control** of the database developer. Even if a particular UID is supposed to be unique and not supposed to ever change, that can seldom be guaranteed. I have been bitten in the past when values that were never supposed to change... changed. With that said, I will return to 'Test Mode'.

Validating the logical data model

Logical models are always created as a prelude to a constructing a physical model. Once the design of a new database has progressed to the point of planning the physical implementation, the logical model diagram must be converted to a physical model diagram. The physical model shows a much more detailed set of specifications for the database tables to be created. Concurrently with changing to the physical model, all of the terms that have been used to this point will change from logical to physical terminology:

- **Entity** => Table
- **Instance** => Row
- **Attribute** => Column
- **Primary unique identifier** => Primary key
- **Secondary unique identifier** => Unique key
- **Relationship** => Foreign key column and constraint

A well-designed logical model will provide most of the details required to create the physical model. In the diagram below, the Aircraft Type entity has five attributes that will map to five table columns. The primary UID will become the primary key of the corresponding table. The four non-key columns are all marked as mandatory in the entity and where therefore be mandatory in the table. Only the data types and sizes required for the table are not included in the entity and this is discussed in the following section.

Logical Model Entity

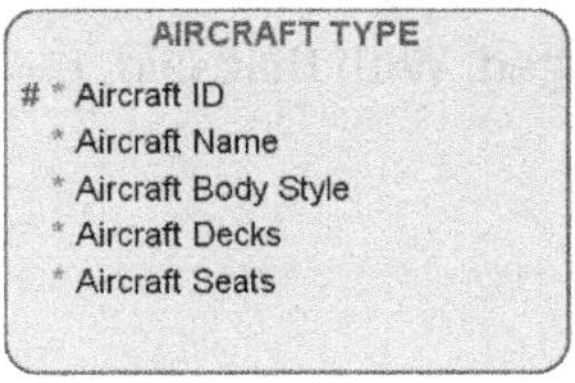

Physical Model Table

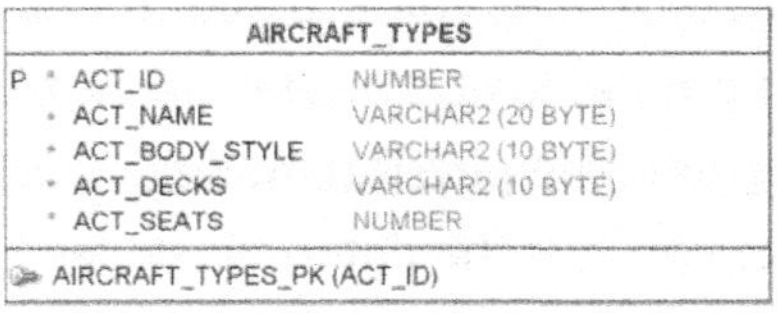

As part of the process of validating the logical model, any uncertainties in the entity relationship diagram should be resolved and the design finalized. Some of the actions that should be performed as part of this validation process include:

- Check that all entities and their relationships have been resolved.
- Compare the ER diagram to the requirements documentation.
- Review the model with the users.
- Make any necessary changes identified in the above steps.
- Get sign offs from all of the stakeholders.

Creating an enterprise data model

An Enterprise Data Model (EDM) is an holistic view of the data produced across an entire organization. The information shown in an EDM is independent of the data source, where it is stored, or how it is accessed. The model is intended to identify and relate all of the information sources important to an organization. The creation of an EDM enables shareable and/or redundant data across the organization to be identified and integrated. Once redundant data sources have been integrated, the result provides a single source of truth. This concept leads to more consistent and accurate data and reduces the errors that can be caused by data disparity.

The first step in creating an EDM is to identify the creators and consumers of data in the organization. Once identified, the business users should be interviewed, as well as any subject matter experts on the data in question. The data designers should use these interviews to identify an initial set of data concepts. Once the initial data concepts across the organization have been identified, later sessions should focus on locating relationships and overlaps between those concepts. Enterprise concept names and definitions are determined from the fashion in which the organization makes use of the data being stored. Concept names should be clear and concise and likewise the concept definitions.

One example of a concept is 'Employee'. One organization I worked for had about a dozen custom applications that had been designed by internal developers. Each application had its own table that stored information about employees for the firm. In order for new hires to be able to use all of the applications, they had to be individually added to each of the tables. This was despite the fact that all of the tables contained almost identical sets of columns. Identifying these tables in an Enterprise Data Model as APPLICATION1_USERS, APPLICATION2_USERS, etc. might not make it clear that the data was redundant. However, identifying all of them as EMPLOYEE_DATA in the EDM would.

An EDM graphically displays concept names and definitions. Concept definitions should be written consistently and begin with "The concept of XXXX describes..." A line is used to represent major business relationships between concepts. It is not necessary (or desirable) to show all of the possible relationships. Adding every relationship for an EDM of any complexity is likely to generate a diagram that is unusable. However, even when relationships that have been identified are not displayed on the model, they should always be defined in the model documentation.

Once an EDM has been created, the design team should go back to the stakeholders in the organization to ensure that they agree that it is both accurate and complete. Once the business has validated the EDM and any necessary adjustments made, a design review should be conducted to verify that it adheres to enterprise standards.

3.3 Interpret logical data models into a physical data model that can be implemented by a particular database management system (DBMS)

Physical database design

A physical database model will contain the table structures, including the column names, data types, and constraints. It will also include any primary keys, foreign keys, and display the relationships between each of the tables. While the physical database model is primarily generated by gathering information from the logical data model, it is possible for the physical data model to have differences from the logical data model depending on the database. While some (probably most) of the required data normalization takes place during the logical design process, it is possible that additional normalization requirements will be found during the physical design process.

One method that can be useful for this is documenting the physical tables using Database Design Language (DBDL). DBDL is a standardized mechanism for representing tables and keys in a relational database. It consists of the table name followed by all of the table columns separated by commas in parentheses and the primary key column(s) underlined. Below this will be listed any columns of the table that can be considered alternate keys, secondary keys, or foreign keys:

- AK identifies alternate keys
- SK identifies secondary keys
- FK identifies foreign keys

The AIRPORTS, AIRCRAFT_TYPES, and AIRCRAFT_FLEET tables in DBDL notation would look like the following:

```
AIRPORTS (APT_ID, APT_NAME, APT_ABBR)
AK   APT_ABBR
SK   APT_NAME

AIRCRAFT_TYPES (ACT_ID, ACT_NAME, ACT_ODY, ACT_DECKS, ACT_SEATS)
SK   ACT_NAME

AIRCRAFT_FLEET (AFL_ID, ACT_ID, APT_ID)
FK   ACT_ID
FK   APT_ID
```

The basic steps to design a physical data model from the logical model are:

1. Convert entities into tables.
2. Convert relationships into foreign keys.
3. Convert attributes into columns.
4. Modify the physical data model based on physical constraints / requirements.

The logical model, by design, does not specify data types for the attributes at all. Attributes do have a domain, which is the set of legal values that can be assigned to them. Domains are analogous to the data types and constraints assigned to a column. However, because the logical model does not have a graphical means for identifying domains in an ERD, the process of identifying data types from a logical model ERD comes down to deciding what the domain is and then picking a compatible data type for the physical model.

For the sake of argument, let us assume that the domains for the below entity are known. Domains, like everything else in the logical model will be logical values rather than physical data types.

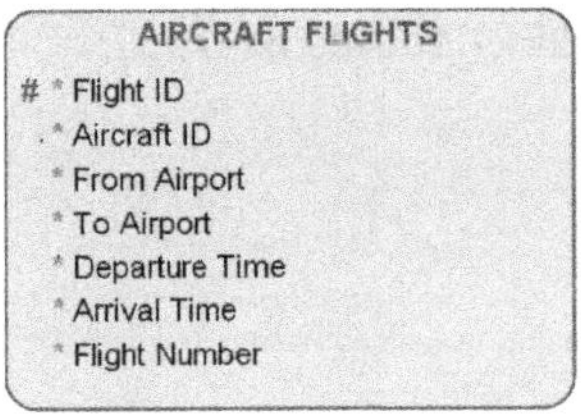

- **Flight ID** -- Integer
- **Aircraft ID** -- Integer
- **From Airport** -- Integer
- **To Airport** -- Integer
- **Departure Time** -- Datetime
- **Arrival Time** -- Datetime
- **Flight Number** -- String

Looking at the above list, you might question why 'Flight number' is set as a string value rather than a number. The answer would be that flight identifiers for airlines often include letters as well as numbers. This would preclude using a numeric field. Unlike the conceptual and logical models, the physical model is database-specific. Just one example of this is that not all relational databases use the same data types. The examples that are used in this section are those available in the Oracle database.

Mapping to the physical model requires that each column be assigned a data type. The destination RDBMS must have data types that map to the chosen domain values. A number of data types also require a maximum length to be specified. For example, a character data type might be specified as CHAR(25). This would indicate that up to 25 characters could be stored in the column. Other data types may require a size specification as well, such as graphic, floating point, and decimal types. For Oracle, the data types that map to Integer, Datetime, and String would be NUMBER, DATE, and VARCHAR2 respectively. After mapping the Aircraft Flights entity to the physical model, the results would look like the below:

AIRCRAFT_FLIGHTS			
P	*	FLT_ID	NUMBER
	*	AFL_ID	NUMBER
	*	APT_ID_FROM	NUMBER
	*	APT_ID_TO	NUMBER
	*	DEPART_TIME	DATE
	*	ARRIVE_TIME	DATE
	*	FLIGHT_ID	VARCHAR2 (20 BYTE)
AIRCRAFT_FLIGHTS_PK (FLT_ID)			

Shown below is a physical model diagram that contains the three tables from the Imaginary Airlines database that correspond to the three entities previously shown for the logical database model of IA. In contrast to the logical model, the columns displayed in the diagram list the data types and sizes. The column names also match the values that will actually be stored in the database (i.e. 'ACT_BODY_STYLE') rather than a human-friendly name (i.e. 'Body Style'). The physical model also includes the primary and foreign key columns.

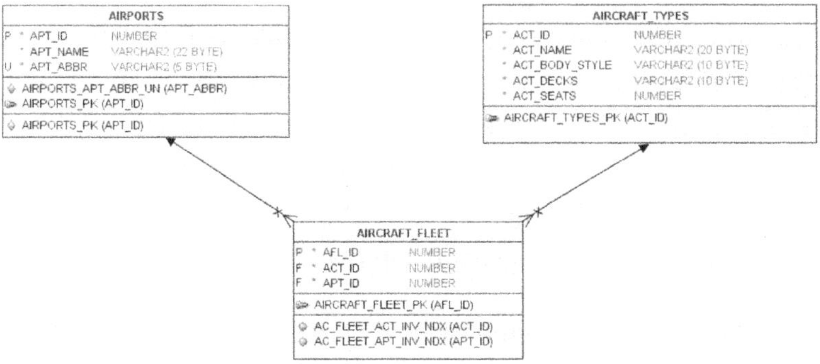

Physical Data Types

Every value contained within a relational database has a data type. The data type associates a given set of properties with the value and causes the database to treat the values differently. For example, it is possible to add, subtract, or multiply two values of the NUMBER data type. However, it is not possible to add two values of a CHAR or VARCHAR2 data type.

Columns are part of the physical model and must account for the type of data to be stored, the amount of space to be allocated for it, and the name that will be recorded for it in the database. For example, the 'Name' attribute in the conceptual model might be a column called ACT_NAME in the physical model, with a VARCHAR2 data type that is limited to 20 bytes. A physical model of the AIRCRAFT TYPE entity might look like the following:

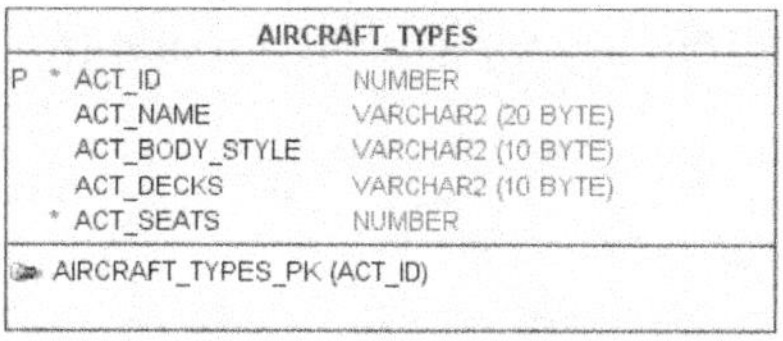

Any time a table is created, every one of its columns must have a data type specified. Data types define the domain of values that each column can contain. Every relational database will have a number of built-in data types. Some databases allow the creation of user-defined types that can be used as data types. Three of the most commonly used data types in the Oracle database are:

- **VARCHAR2(n)** -- Variable-length character string of n characters or bytes.
- **NUMBER** -- Number having optional precision and scale values.
- **DATE** -- This data type contains the datetime fields YEAR, MONTH, DAY, HOUR, MINUTE, and SECOND. It does not have fractional seconds or a time zone.

For the majority of Oracle databases, the above three data types will comprise over ninety percent of the columns. Other database vendors will have three equivalent types that make up a similar percentage. Most of the other data types available are used for data that is seldom seen in most database applications. Some of the other types that you may encounter if you use Oracle include the following.

- **TIMESTAMP** -- This data type contains the datetime fields YEAR, MONTH, DAY, HOUR, MINUTE, and SECOND. It contains fractional seconds but does not have a time zone.
- **CHAR(n)** -- Fixed-length character data of length n bytes or characters.
- **CLOB** -- A character large object containing single-byte or multibyte characters.
- **BLOB** -- A binary large object.

- **BFILE** -- Contains a locator to a large binary file stored outside the database.

Creating enterprise constraints

There are several different types of integrity that must ideally be maintained in a relational database. Constraints are part of the physical model that are used to ensure that data integrity is not lost. While constraints are created in the physical model, it is during the logical process that the work of defining constraints begins. The various type of data integrity include the following:

- **Entity integrity** – Tables must have a primary key and no part of a primary key can be NULL. This is because the primary key value is used to identify individual rows in a table. If NULL values were allowed for primary keys, it would prevent those rows from being indentified.
- **Referential integrity** –- Foreign keys must match an existing primary key value or else be NULL.
- **Domain integrity** -– Columns must contain only values that are consistent with their defined data format and length. Other domain integrity rules can include being unique within the table, or not NULL.
- **User-defined integrity** -– All data stored in the database must comply with pre-defined business rules.

Constraints are database objects that are used to restrict (constrain) the data allowed into table columns. They are essentially rules that must be met in order for a value to be acceptable. There are several different kinds of constraints available in relational databases:

- **PRIMARY KEY** – The primary key of a table defines a column, or set of columns that must be unique for every row of a table. To satisfy a primary key constraint, none of the column(s) making up the key may be NULL, and the combination of values in the column(s) must be unique. A table can have only a single primary key constraint defined (all other constraint types can exist multiple times in the same table). Primary key constraints are used to maintain entity integrity.

- **FOREIGN KEY** – Foreign keys are also referred to as Referential Integrity constraints. A foreign key constraint ties a column value in one table to a primary or unique key value in another. Values may not be inserted in the table with the foreign key constraint that do not exist in the referenced key.
- **UNIQUE** – A unique key defines a column or set of columns that must be unique for every row of a table. Unlike a primary key constraint, the UNIQUE constraint does not prevent NULL values in the columns(s) comprising the constraint.
- **NOT NULL** – A NOT NULL constraint prevents a table column from having NULL values. If a column with a UNIQUE constraint is also defined as NOT NULL, it will have the same restrictive behavior as a PRIMARY KEY.
- **CHECK** – Check constraints allow for custom conditions to be specified for a column. The conditions must evaluate to TRUE for the operation altering the column value to succeed. Check constraints are often used to maintain user-defined data integrity.

Primary Keys

For a table to conform to the relational model, every row must be unique without exception. The vast majority of tables have multiple columns. Therefore it is only necessary that a given row not match every single column value with every single column value of a second row in order to be unique. While not absolutely required, it is standard practice (and good database design) for every table in a relational database to have a primary key associated with it.

A primary key is selected by the database designer as a column or set of columns that uniquely identify rows in a table. A table may have more than one column or more than one set of columns that could uniquely identify a given row. However a table can have only a single primary key designated for it. A primary key value must not be null. If the primary key consists of several columns, **none** of those columns can have a null value for any row. There are three different flavors of keys that are possible:

Simple Key

A simple key consists of a single column that uniquely identifies each row of the table. A simple key cannot be broken down into smaller elements. For example, the APT_ABBR column in the AIRPORTS table is the three-letter code for each airport. This number is unique worldwide and could be used to uniquely identify a particular airport. APT_ABBR is a single column and therefore would be a simple key. No two airports would have the same three-letter abbreviation.

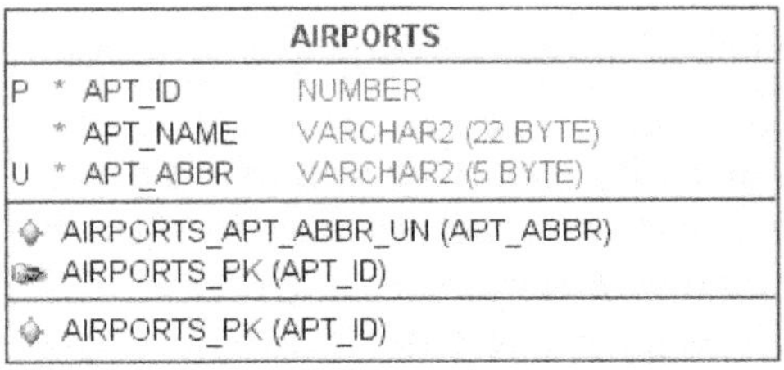

Compound Key

A compound key consists of two or more columns that when combined uniquely identify a row. Each column that makes up a compound key is a simple key in its own right. The AIRCRAFT_FLEET table contains the ACT_ID column (which is the primary key for the AIRCRAFT_TYPES table) and the APT_ID column (which is the primary key for the AIRPORTS table). If these two columns were used as the primary key for the AIRCRAFT_FLEET table, it would be a compound key. Each of the elements of the compound key is also a simple key when referencing either an airport or an aircraft type.

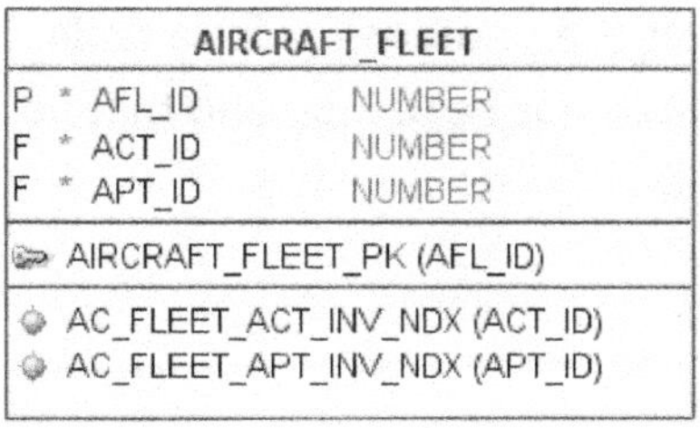

Composite Key

Like a compound key, a composite key consists of two or more columns that uniquely identify a row. A composite key differs from a compound key in that one or more of the columns which make up the key, are not simple keys in their own right. An example composite key could be made using the AIRCRAFT_FLIGHTS table. The FLIGHT_ID field for this table is not unique across all rows. Imaginary Airlines (like most airlines) want flight numbers that are short enough for passengers to remember them. Flight numbers are therefore unique only across a given timeframe. In order to make each row unique, a composite key for this table would have to include at least the FLIGHT_ID and DEPART_DATE fields. Imaginary Airlines will never duplicate IDs for flights leaving on the same day. When combined, the two fields make up a unique identifier, but neither of the two columns by themselves is a simple key because the departure date or flight ID in isolation could not be used to uniquely identify rows in any table.

AIRCRAFT_TYPE	FROM_AIRPORT	TO_AIRPORT	DEPART_DATE	ARRIVE_DATE	FLIGHT_ID
Boeing 767	Miami, FL	Orlando, FL	2-Jan-14	2-Jan-14	Flight 010217
Boeing 767	Dallas/Fort Worth	Orlando, FL	2-Jan-14	2-Jan-14	Flight 010917
Boeing 767	Miami, FL	Orlando, FL	1-May-14	1-May-14	Flight 010117
Boeing 737	Jacksonville, FL	Atlanta, GA	11-Jul-14	11-Jul-14	Flight 031116
Boeing 737	Miami, FL	Atlanta, GA	18-Jul-14	18-Jul-14	Flight 031811
Boeing 767	Miami, FL	Orlando, FL	1-Jan-15	1-Jan-15	Flight 010117
Boeing 757	Miami, FL	Atlanta, GA	7-Jul-15	7-Jul-15	Flight 040720
Boeing 747	Orlando, FL	Dallas/Fort Worth	8-Dec-15	8-Dec-15	Flight 070812

Any of the three types of keys can be used as the primary key for a table. The only requirements for a primary key are that it be unique and that no element of it contains a NULL value.

Referential Integrity Constraints

When a referential integrity constraint is specified between two tables, it maintains the consistency among rows between the two tables with matching column values. The master table in a foreign key relationship is the one where the column(s) forming the relationship compose the table's primary key. The other table in the relationship is known as the child table. Relationship maintenance takes the form of rules:

1. A row cannot be deleted from the master table while matching records continue to exist in the child table.
2. It is not possible to enter a value in the foreign key field of the child table that does not exist in the primary key of the master table.
3. It is possible to enter a NULL value in the foreign key of the child table (unless the FK columns have a NOT NULL constraint). This will produce a row in the child table that is unrelated to any row of the parent table.

The first rule can be enforced in different ways depending on how the foreign key is configured. There are three potential behaviors for a foreign key constraint:

- **CASCADE RESTRICT** -- When a foreign key is set to restrict mode, deletes from the parent table are prevented from occurring any time there are matching records in the child table.
- **CASCADE DELETE** -- When a foreign key is set to delete mode, deletes from the parent table are cascaded to any matching records in the child table.
- **CASCADE UPDATE** -- When a foreign key is set to update mode, deletes from the parent table causes any matching records in the child table to have the foreign key columns set to some value. The

value might be NULL or it might be some default value depending on the constraint. UPDATE operations against the parent table key will 'cascade' by changing the value in the child table to match.

Relationship mapping to constraints

The columns that act as the foreign key in a child table will always match the column (for a single column primary key) or columns (for a composite primary key) of the parent table. The foreign key constraint will ensure that any values placed in the columns already exist in the parent table. If a delete operation is executed against one or more rows in the parent table that have child records associated with them, the database will take one of several potential actions to ensure that referential integrity is maintained. This might involve preventing the delete from occurring, cascading the delete to remove the child records, or setting the values in the foreign key column(s) of child records to NULL.

In the preceding chapters of this guide, a number of different relationship specifiers have been discussed: optionality, cardinality, transferrability, etc. When mapping the ERD from the logical to physical models, those relationships become foreign key constraints. However, foreign key constraints do not enforce all of the restrictions that can be specified in an ERD. The remainder will require additional constraints or code to enforce in the database. In order to determine whether this will be required, you must understand what exactly is required by a given relationship and what portion of that requirement will be fulfilled by a foreign key constraint.

Optionality

A relationship can be optional on one side, both sides, or neither side. When a foreign key constraint is created in a table, it can be made mandatory or optional to match the relationship type. If the foreign key constraint is optional -- all that it does is ensure that IF a value is placed in that column, the matching value exists in the parent table's primary key. If the constraint is set to require a value, it ensures both that a value is entered in the column and that it exists in the parent table.

However, a foreign key constraint can only enforce this from the table on which the constraint is created. For example, in the below diagram, there is a mandatory one-to-one relationship between the Aircraft Fleet and Cabin Fitting entities. A foreign key constraint would be created on the table which represents the Cabin Fitting entity. This constraint can prevent the creation of a new row in the table when no corresponding row exists in the AIRCRAFT_FLEET table. However, it cannot prevent a new row from being created in the AIRCRAFT_FLEET where the mandatory matching row is not also created in the CABIN_FITTINGS table. In order to properly match the specifications in the ERD, the database would require code that automatically created a record in CABIN_FITTINGS every time a new row is added to the AIRCRAFT_FLEET table.

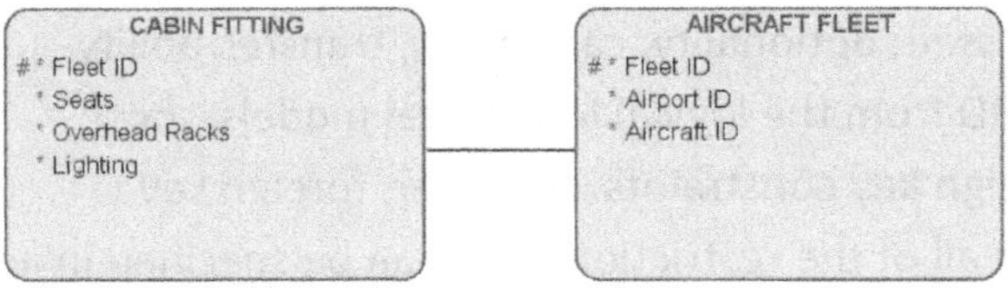

Cardinality

Using the same diagram from above, the ERD specification is for a one-to-one relationship. For the AIRCRAFT_FLEET table, there will never be any more than one row with a given primary key value by definition. However, the foreign key constraint only requires that rows added to CABIN_FITTINGS have a matching PK value in AIRCRAFT_FLEET. A foreign key constraint can not prevent more than one matching rows from being added to the child table. In order to enforce a one-to-one relationship on the child side, the foreign key column(s) must have a unique key constraint added in addition to the foreign key constraint.

Nontransferable Relationships

When the logical model contains a nontransferable relationship, it indicates that the foreign key column in the database table cannot be updated. Perhaps it is not allowed for cabin fittings to be moved from one aircraft in the fleet to another as per the below diagram. Once again, a foreign key constraint does not have the ability to enforce this restriction. Enforcing this rule will require code to be created that will ensure that rows in the CABIN_FITTINGS table are not transferred to a different aircraft in the fleet after they are created.

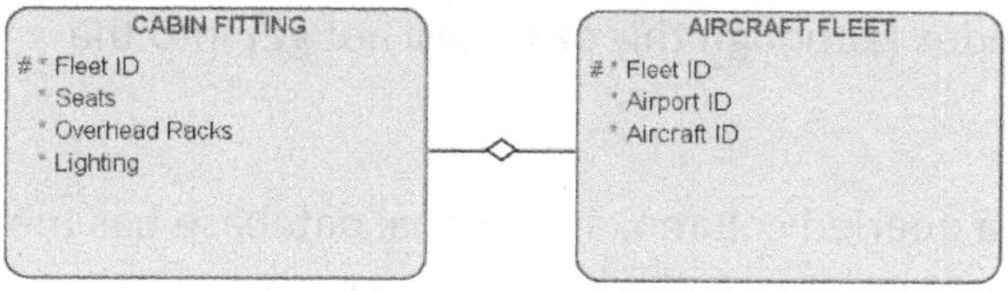

Barred Relationships

As with any one-to-many relationship, barred relationships will be mapped as a foreign key column on the many side. However, the column(s) making up the foreign key column will also be part of the primary key for the child table. Because they are part of the primary key, none of the foreign key column values can be NULL.

Using secondary indexes

Any table in a relational database that has a primary key will automatically have at least the index that is used to enforce that primary key. It is possible to create indexes for additional columns in a given tables beyond the column(s) used for the primary key. Indexes are schema objects that store pointers to table rows based on data in the table. Indexes can be used to guarantee that the value(s) in a given column or set of columns are unique in that table. In this role, they act as constraints. Indexes can also be use to improve the response time of queries against a table.

When the conditions of a query reference only columns that have no indexes, a relational database must scan every single row in the table in order to ensure that the correct data is returned. This is known as a full table scan. To be fair, while it is often desirable to avoid a full table scan, there are many times when performing one can be faster than performing the same query using an index (although this exam will not get into the reasons why that is).

When indexes do exist on a queried column, a relational database has the option of using them and potentially speeding up data retrieval and reducing disk I/O. Creating or dropping an index has no direct impact on the table itself. The reverse is not true. Dropping a table will also drop any indexes that have previously been created on the table.

Indexes contain an entry for each value that appears in the indexed column(s) of the table. Each index entry contains a locator to the block(s) in the data file containing the row(s) with that value and provide direct, fast access to them. It's possible to have multiple indexes on any given table. A query that includes an indexed column in a WHERE clause might see a performance benefit. However, INSERT UPDATE and DELETE operations that affect any indexed columns will be slower because in addition to updating the table, the database must perform a second operation to maintain the index. In addition, indexes consume additional space in the database – especially multi-column indexes on large tables.

There are several rule-of-thumb guidelines on index creation. Indexing every column in every table is certainly not a good idea. Indexing no columns in any table is likewise generally not a good idea. Determining which columns to index in each table is the key to getting the best performance boost possible from indexing.

Some of the indicators that you might want an index built on a column include:

- The column has a broad range of values.
- The table is large and queries tend to retrieve a small percentage of the table rows (less than 2-4%.
- The column is often used in a WHERE clause or as a JOIN column.
- The column is used as a foreign key to another table.

Signs that you might NOT want an index built on a column:

- The column is seldom used as a query condition or JOIN column.
- The table is frequently updated.
- The table is small or most queries return more than 2-4% of the table rows.
- The columns are generally referenced as part of an expression.
- The table is often updates using batch operations.

Denormalization

One of the primary goals of a relational database is to store data in a completely normalized format. The question then is -- why is there a chapter on denormalization? Essentially, denormalization is sometimes performed to address performance or scalability issues that occur in a relational database.

Because a fully normalized database can store related pieces of information in multiple separate logical tables, completing a database query often requires multiple join operations in order to complete. Given a sufficiently large number of joins and rows, this operation can become unacceptably slow.

This problem can be addressed using one of two methods. The preferred means is to leave the logical data design fully normalized and store a set of redundant (denormalized) data that is used to optimize the performance of queries against the data. When this redundant data exists, it must be kept consistent with what exists in the logical data design or else queries against the data can be inconsistent. Several RDBMS vendors, including Oracle, Microsoft SQL Server, and PostgreSQL have built-in capabilities for doing this. Materialized views in Oracle and PostgreSQL or indexed views in MS SQL Server are designed for just this purpose.

The other option is to denormalize the logical data design. While this can improve query response, the database developer must ensure that the denormalization does not result in data inconsistencies. By definition, denormalization means that the same data now appears in multiple locations. Constraints must be added to the database to ensure that redundant copies of information are kept synchronized. This action is liable to slow down the performance of DML operations against the denormalized tables in order to improve the performance of SELECT operations.

A database should always be fully normalized during the initial design. Denormalization should only be considered if it is determined that there is a performance problem introduced by normalization that must be addressed.

Creating user views

There are two ways in which the term 'views' can be taken in the context of database design. There are logical views which are developed as a late step in the logical design process. There is a physical database object called a view which will be created when the database application is built.

Logical Views

As part of the logical design process, entities from the conceptual view were broken into pieces in order to normalize the data. However, this is not how users will expect to access the data once a database application has been created. In order to logically recombine the very entities that were split up during the normalization process in order to create 'User Views' that can display data in the form that users expect/need it to be in when they are performing their duties. These logical views will later be created in the database application as database objects (discussed below). The second example in the next section that builds the view called AIRCRAFT_FLEET_V is a perfect example of creating a logical view of the data that presents information in the fashion that users expect to see.

Database Objects

Views in relational databases are essentially SQL queries that have been saved to the data dictionary. Sometimes referred to as 'virtual' tables, they act as a logical table in the database and can be queried via SQL as such. No data is physically stored in views. The rows that they return when queried have their source in the table or tables that are referenced in the SQL of the stored query that makes up the view. These are generally referred to as base tables. Views allow administrators to fine-tune the presentation of data that is made visible to users. They are used for many purposes, including:

- **Formatting or generating data** -- The query that makes up the view can be used to format the data in existing columns. For example, a view against a table containing employees might concatenate a FIRST_NAME and LAST_NAME column into a single column in the view called EMPLOYEE_NAME. The hire date might be formatted to a specific date style or the salary field formatted to add currency symbols.
- **Security** -- Views can add a level of data security by restricting access to a predetermined set of rows or columns of the base table. For example, instead of granting users access to a base table (which allows them to see all columns and rows in that table), an administrator might create a view that SELECTs a subset of the columns and/or has a WHERE clause that restricts the rows available. The administrator can then grant access on the view to a user rather than to the base table. Any portion of the table not returned by the view will be completely inaccessible to the user.
- **Hide data complexity** -- A side effect of data normalization is that it is often necessary to JOIN multiple tables together in order to return the data needed by a given operation. Views can be created that logically re-combine the data that the normalization process separated. This makes it simpler for users (or applications) to access required data. Because the view is a logical re-combination of the data rather than a physical recombination, this activity is not the same as denormalization.
- **Alter Perspectives** -- A view can appear completely different from the base table(s) it is created against. The column names and order can be tailored to meet the needs of the users or applications that access it without requiring any changes to the base table.
- **Provide structural isolation** -- Organizational requirements sometimes force the physical structure of tables to be altered. This might include adding columns, changing column names, etc. This can introduce defects into applications and code that reference those tables. If the applications instead reference a view of the table, it is likely that the physical change to the table can be hidden by the logical structure of the view. This can sidestep the possibility of introducing defects into a production application.

In order to create a view, a given user must have the CREATE VIEW privilege for the schema where the view will be created. In addition, the user must have SELECT privileges on the table or tables that are included in the SQL of the view statement.

An example of using views to enhance application security is below. Imaginary Airlines would like to allow employees to locate the job titles of other people at the company easily. However, they cannot give them direct access to the EMPLOYEES table because it contains salary data. The following query creates a view that shows only employees and their job title. Access to the view can be granted freely without making salary data visible:

EMPLOYEES			
P	*	EMP_ID	NUMBER
		AFL_ID	NUMBER
		EMP_FIRST	VARCHAR2 (10 BYTE)
	*	EMP_LAST	VARCHAR2 (10 BYTE)
		EMP_JOB	VARCHAR2 (10 BYTE)
		EMP_SUPERVISOR	NUMBER
		SALARY	NUMBER
		START_DATE	DATE
EMPLOYEES_PK (EMP_ID)			
EMP_LAST_NDX (EMP_LAST)			
EMP_LAST_FIRST_NDX (EMP_LAST, EMP_FIRST)			

```
CREATE VIEW employee_jobs_v
AS
SELECT emp_first FIRST_NAME,
       emp_last  LAST_NAME,
       emp_job   JOB_TITLE
FROM   employees;

SELECT *
FROM   employee_jobs_v
WHERE  job_title = 'Pilot';

FIRST_NAME LAST_NAME  JOB_TITLE
---------- ---------- ----------
John       Jones      Pilot
Top        Gun        Pilot
Phil       McCoy      Pilot
James      Thomas     Pilot
John       Picard     Pilot
Luke       Skytalker  Pilot
Dell       Aptop      Pilot
Noh        Kia        Pilot
```

For a more complex example of the use of views, consider the AIRCRAFT_FLEET table in the image below. The table exists as an intersection table between AIRPORTS and AIRCRAFT_TYPES to show planes in the Imaginary Airlines fleet by type and home airport. The actual data in the AIRCRAFT_FLEET table is meaningless to uses since it contains only numbers from the artificial keys in the other two tables.

AIRPORTS

APT_ID	APT_NAME	APT_ABBR
1	Orlando, FL	MCO
2	Atlanta, GA	ATL
3	Miami, FL	MIA
4	Jacksonville, FL	JAX
5	Dallas/Fort Worth	DFW
7	Houston, TX	IAH

AIRCRAFT_TYPES

ACT_ID	ACT_NAME	ACT_BODY_STYLE	ACT_DECKS	ACT_SEATS
1	Boeing 747	Wide	Double	416
2	Boeing 767	Wide	Single	350
3	Boeing 737	Narrow	Single	200
4	Boeing 757	Narrow	Single	240
5	Boeing 777	Wide	Single	407
6	Boeing 787	Wide	Single	296

AIRCRAFT_FLEET

AFL_ID	ACT_ID	APT_ID
1	2	1
2	2	1
3	3	2
4	4	2
5	1	3
6	1	3
7	1	5
8	2	5

In order to get useful information about Imaginary Airlines' fleet, a query joining all three tables together is required. This is a perfect opportunity to use a view to reduce data complexity. The following statement creates a view that joins the three tables together, combines columns from them, and renames the columns to a more user-friendly style:

```
CREATE OR REPLACE VIEW aircraft_fleet_v
AS
SELECT apt_name        AS AIRPORT,
       apt_abbr        AS ABBR,
       act_name        AS AIRCRAFT,
       act_body_style  AS BODY_STYLE,
       act_decks       AS DECKS,
       act_seats       AS SEATS
FROM airports apt
     INNER JOIN aircraft_fleet afl
     ON apt.apt_id = afl.apt_id
     INNER JOIN aircraft_types act
     ON act.act_id = afl.act_id;
```

Once the view as been created, it can be queried as if it were a table to return the fleet data in a much more useful fashion:

```
SELECT airport, abbr, aircraft, body_style, decks, seats
FROM   aircraft_fleet_v;

AIRPORT              ABBR  AICRAFT      BODY_STYLE DECKS   SEATS
-------------------- ----- ------------ ---------- ------- ------
Dallas/Fort Worth    DFW   Boeing 747   Wide       Double     416
Miami, FL            MIA   Boeing 747   Wide       Double     416
Miami, FL            MIA   Boeing 747   Wide       Double     416
Dallas/Fort Worth    DFW   Boeing 767   Wide       Single     350
Orlando, FL          MCO   Boeing 767   Wide       Single     350
Orlando, FL          MCO   Boeing 767   Wide       Single     350
Atlanta, GA          ATL   Boeing 737   Narrow     Single     200
Atlanta, GA          ATL   Boeing 757   Narrow     Single     240
```

Designing database access rules

In order for a RDBMS to be a viable platform for enterprise databases, the data must be secure. The sum total of the data within it should not be freely available to anyone that can log in to the database. Relational databases maintain security through the use of user privileges. By default, newly created users in a database have no privileges assigned to them. This ensures that the database administrator can grant them only those rights which they require in order to perform their duties. The commands that are used to control privileges within the database are known as Data Control Language (DCL). As mentioned earlier, DCL is a subset of DDL and not all database vendors distinguish between the two.

There are two broad classes of privileges that can be granted to a user or role:

System Privileges – Provide the ability to perform a task that has a scope beyond that of a single database object. Many the system privileges have a scope of the entire database, for example ALTER USER or CREATE ROLLBACK SEGMENT. Others have a scope that is just for the schema of the user who has been granted the privilege, for example CREATE TABLE or CREATE PROCEDURE.

Object Privileges – Provide the ability to perform a task on a specific database object. For example, GRANT SELECT ON employees.

Some examples of System Privileges are:

- **CREATE TABLE** -- Create a table in the grantee's schema.
- **CREATE ANY TABLE** -- Create a table in any schema.
- **ALTER ANY TABLE** -- Alter any table or view in any schema.
- **DELETE ANY TABLE** -- Delete rows from tables in any schema.
- **DROP ANY TABLE** -- Drop (or truncate) tables in any schema.
- **INSERT ANY TABLE** -- Insert rows into tables in any schema.
- **CREATE ANY INDEX** Create an index on any table in any schema.
- **ALTER ANY INDEX** Alter indexes in any schema.

Some examples of Object Privileges are:

- **ALTER** – Right to use ALTER TABLE to change a given table.
- **INDEX** – Right to use the CREATE INDEX command on a given table.
- **INSERT** – Right to INSERT new rows into a given table.
- **SELECT** – Right to SELECT data from a given table.
- **UPDATE** – Right to UPDATE data in a given table.
- **DELETE** – Right to use DELETE rows from a given table.

System level privileges by their nature are often less restrictive than object privileges. This is especially true when the ANY keyword is used to grant system privileges across all schemas of the database. Unless a user has a job role that requires the level of access conferred by system privileges, it is best to grant rights at an object level. Once a user has been granted access to all schemas, it is difficult for the database administrator to keep track of cases where they may have access to something that they really should not.

WITH ADMIN OPTION

System privileges may optionally be made using the WITH ADMIN option (i.e. GRANT ALTER ANY TABLE WITH ADMIN OPTION). This option allows the user granted this privilege to grant it to other users in turn. In fact, they can grant the privilege to a third user 'WITH ADMIN OPTION' who could in turn grant it to a fourth and so on. The admin option is very dangerous. This is not something that should be granted except to highly privileged database administrators.

WITH GRANT OPTION

Object privileges have a similar clause called the WITH GRANT OPTION. When an object privilege is granted to a user with this option, that user can grant the object privilege to other users. The "with grant" option is not nearly as dangerous as the "with admin" option, but it is still not something to be done lightly.

GROUPS/ROLES

Most relational databases have a concept called either a Group or a Role (the word 'Role' will be used to mean either from this point forward). A role acts as a container to hold a set of privileges. Roles can be granted to users in the same fashion as privileges. However, the role is not in and of itself a privilege. When created, a new role contains no privileges and granting it to a user would confer no additional rights within the database. Once privileges have been added to a role and the role granted to a user, the user can then make use of the privileges that have been granted to the role.

The purpose of roles is to create sets of common privileges together so that they can easily be granted to individuals. If everyone in an organization with a hundred people need the same ten privileges. It is much easier to grant the ten privileges to a role, then the one role to those hundred people.

Application Testing

When testing an application, whether it is for a databases or any type of software, the method of testing can be classified as either black box or white box. The concept is that when performing black box testing, the person performing the test does not have any visibility into the processing of the application being tested. They put input into one side of a 'black box' and get output from the other side, without knowing what happened in-between. In white-box testing, the person has complete visibility into the application processing. When they provide input into the 'white box', they know and/or can see each step of the processing that occurs until they receive their ouput. Some attributes of white-box and black box testing are:

White Box Testing

- Internal structure of code is known to the person performing the test.
- Performed by software developers.
- Implementation Knowledge is required.
- Programming Knowledge is required
- Applicable to low-level testing such as Unit or Integration testing.
- Concentrates on testing the program code of the system being tested.

Black Box Testing

- Internal structure of code is not known to the person performing the test.
- Performed by users.
- Implementation Knowledge is not required.
- Programming Knowledge is not required.
- Applicable to high-level testing such as System or Acceptance testing.
- Concentrates on the functionality of the system being tested.

Domain 4: Structured Query Language (SQL)

4.1 Identify SQL commands and syntax

Using Structured Query Language

SQL was introduced early in this guide. It is the standard language use to work with relational databases and it is almost impossible to deal with one to any degree without requiring a reasonable level of familiarity with it. SQL is used by database administrators, developers, architects, data analysts, business intelligence specialists, and more. If you do not currently know much about the language but plan to work with databases, you should make learning it a high priority. There are a number of terms that will be associated with SQL statements throughout the text:

- **Alias** – Aliases are used to provide an alternate (usually shorter or more readable) name for an item in the select list or for a table reference. Aliases improve readability of the statement and are required for certain operations.
- **Keyword** – Keywords are defined individual elements of a SQL statement (SELECT, FROM, WHERE, GROUP BY, etc.)
- **Clause** – A clause is a subset of a SQL statement that is tied to a keyword. For example, "SELECT first_name, last_name" is a SELECT clause.
- **Expression** – An expression is an element in a select list that is not a column. It may or may not contain a column. For example, given the clause "SELECT last_name, first_name, first_name || ' ' || last_name", two elements in the clause (first_name and last_name) are columns, and (first_name || ' ' || last_name) is an expression.
- **Literal** – An element in the SELECT list that will be returned from the query unchanged. For example, "SELECT 'Fred' FROM dual;' would return the text literal 'Fred'.
- **Statement** – A statement is a combination of two or more clauses that form a complete SQL operation. At the bare minimum a SQL statement must include a SELECT clause and a FROM clause.

Expressions

Expressions in the select list of a SQL statement include essentially everything except a bare column name. They could be literals, column data that has been modified by operators, or SQL functions.

Text Literals -- Use to specify values whenever 'string' appears in the syntax of expressions, conditions, SQL functions, and SQL statements. Text literals are always surrounded by single quotation marks.

```
SELECT 'Fred' AS STRING_LIT
FROM dual;
STRING_LIT
----------
Fred
```

Text literals can be used to provide context or formatting to the data being selected from the table.

```
SELECT emp_last || ', ' || emp_first || ' (' || emp_job ||
       ') started on ' || start_date AS EMP_BIO
FROM   employees
WHERE  emp_job = 'Pilot';

EMP_BIO
--------------------------------------------------
Jones, John (Pilot) started on 10-APR-95
Gun, Top (Pilot) started on 13-OCT-96
McCoy, Phil (Pilot) started on 09-JUN-96
Thomas, James (Pilot) started on 12-MAY-99
Picard, John (Pilot) started on 11-NOV-01
Skytalker, Luke (Pilot) started on 10-SEP-02
Aptop, Dell (Pilot) started on 22-AUG-03
Kia, Noh (Pilot) started on 07-JUL-04
```

Numeric Literals -- Use numeric literal notation to specify fixed and floating-point numbers.

```
SELECT 14.5 AS NUM_LIT
FROM dual;

NUM_LIT
-------
14.5
```

Note: All of the SQL examples used in this study guide were performed in an Oracle database. While I have written all of the SQL using the ANSI standard, it is possible that one or more of the statements will not work as written here if executed verbatim in an RDBMS from a different vendor. Likewise, the SQL you will encounter on the exam may have slight syntax differences, but the statements will still be completely recognizable.

4.2 Create statements using Data Definition Language (DDL)

Data definition language

As briefly discussed in an earlier chapter, Data Definition Language (DDL) statements are used to make changes to the data dictionary. The three most common commands performed in DDL are to CREATE, ALTER, and DROP objects. That said, there are dozens of types of objects and hundreds of different ways to mix and match the options available in DDL commands affecting them. In addition, while DML commands are fairly standard across relational databases that adhere to ANSI standards, the commonality of DDL commands is much lower. Therefore, any DDL presented in this guide will be that of a specific RDBMS (Oracle in this case) and may not match closely with comparable statements from other database vendors. That said, this chapter will present some examples of CREATE, ALTER, and DROP operations.

CREATE

The CREATE TABLE statement of Oracle has a dizzying number of options. Given the uncertainties noted in the paragraph above, I doubt that you will be required to know any of the specific options. However, at the very minimum for a table, you must specify a table name, and one column. The skeleton of the minimum CREATE TABLE syntax in is:

```
CREATE TABLE table_name (col1 datatype [, col2 datatype…]);
```

At its most basic, an Oracle create table statement would look something like the following:

```
CREATE TABLE ocp_example (
  ocp_id                    NUMBER,
  ocp_name                  VARCHAR2(20),
  ocp_date                  DATE);
```

The statement can be broken down into the reserved words CREATE and TABLE, followed by a name for the table, and the column list. The column list must be enclosed in parentheses, and contain column name/data type pairs separated by commas. The table name and the column names must follow the naming rules of the target RDBMS. The SQL statement should be terminated by a semicolon.

A slightly more complex CREATE TABLE statement is below. In addition to defining the column data types, it adds a NOT NULL constraint to the EMP_LAST column and sets the EMP_ID column as the primary key of the table. In addition, it creates a default for the START_DATE column of SYSDATE.

```
CREATE TABLE employees (
  emp_id                  NUMBER,
  afl_id                  NUMBER,
  emp_first               VARCHAR2(10),
  emp_last                VARCHAR2(10) NOT NULL,
  emp_job                 VARCHAR2(10),
  emp_supervisor          NUMBER,
  salary                  NUMBER,
  start_date              DATE DEFAULT SYSDATE,
    PRIMARY KEY (EMP_ID)
);
```

Constraints in Oracle are created by one of two methods. They can be created simultaneously with the table during the CREATE TABLE statement. Alternately they can be created on a table that already exists using the ALTER TABLE statement. There is no such thing as a 'CREATE CONSTRAINT' command. The SQL statement below creates a table with two constraints:

```
CREATE TABLE aircraft_types (
  act_id              NUMBER,
  act_name            VARCHAR2(20),
  act_body_style      VARCHAR2(10),
  act_decks           NUMBER,
  act_seats           NUMBER  NOT NULL
    CONSTRAINT ac_type_pk PRIMARY KEY (act_id)
);
```

Beyond creating the table and columns with associated data types, it contains the instructions for adding two constraints.

- The **act_seats** column has been assigned a NOT NULL constraint. If an insert to this table doesn't reference this column, or references it but attempts to add a NULL value to the column, an error will occur. Because no name was specified for the constraint, Oracle will give it a system-generated name. This is an in-line constraint definition because it is added in the same line as the column. NULL and NOT NULL constraints **must** be defined in-line during a CREATE or ALTER TABLE statements.
- The **act_id** column has been assigned a primary key constraint, and the constraint given the name 'ac_type_pk'. Oracle will create an index of the same name to enforce the primary key constraint. This constraint has been defined out-of-line.

In the example above, the PRIMARY KEY constraint definition was listed at the end of the statement rather than with the column. This is known as out-of-line constraint definition. The following is equivalent to the first SQL statement, with the primary key constraint being defined inline. The end result of a constraint defined inline or out-of-line is identical.

The next CREATE TABLE statement will create the AIRPORTS table. In addition to creating a PRIMARY KEY constraint, the statement adds a UNIQUE constraint on the APT_ABBR column. No two airports may use the same three-letter airport code.

```
CREATE TABLE airports (
 apt_id      NUMBER NOT NULL,
 apt_name    VARCHAR2(22) NOT NULL,
 apt_abbr    VARCHAR2(5) NOT NULL,
   UNIQUE (apt_abbr),
   CONSTRAINT airports_pk PRIMARY KEY (apt_id)
);
```

The final create statement below generates three constraints, a PRIMARY KEY once again, and two FOREIGN KEY constraints that reference the AIRPORTS and AIRCRAFT_TYPES tables respectively. The two FK constraints make the AIRCRAFT_FLEET into an intersection table to support the many-to-many relationship between AIRPORTS and AIRCRAFT_TYPES.

```
CREATE TABLE aircraft_fleet (
 afl_id      NUMBER NOT NULL,
 act_id      NUMBER NOT NULL,
 apt_id      NUMBER NOT NULL,
 last_pmcs   DATE,
   CONSTRAINT aircraft_fleet_pk PRIMARY KEY (afl_id),
   CONSTRAINT aircraft_fleet_apt_fk FOREIGN KEY (apt_id)
      REFERENCES airports (apt_id) ENABLE,
   CONSTRAINT aircraft_fleet_act_fk FOREIGN KEY (act_id)
      REFERENCES aircraft_types (act_id) ENABLE
);
```

Once all three statements have been executed, the resulting table structure matches the physical model that has been shown throughout this guide:

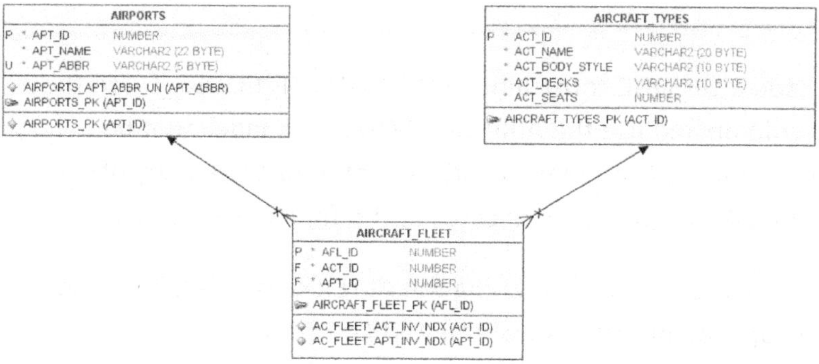

ALTER

The ALTER command allows changes to be made to existing objects in the data dictionary. In Oracle, the basic command consists of the ALTER command followed by an object type, object name, and the actions to be performed:

```
ALTER object_type object_name [instructions];
```

In the section above were examples of constraints being generated at the time of table creation. It is also possible to add constraints to a table after it has been created using the ALTER TABLE statement. To add a NOT NULL constraint to a column in an existing table, the command would be of the form:

```
ALTER TABLE employees MODIFY (last_name NOT NULL);

table EMPLOYEES altered.
```

This would add a unnamed NOT NULL constraint to the LAST_NAME column.

```
CREATE UNIQUE INDEX airport_codes_uk ON airports (apt_abbr);
unique index AIRPORT_CODES_UK created.

ALTER TABLE airports MODIFY (apt_abbr CONSTRAINT airport_codes_uk
                             UNIQUE USING INDEX airport_codes_uk);
table AIRPORTS altered.
```

This would add a UNIQUE constraint called AIRPORT_CODES_UK to the APT_ABBR column and use the AIRPORT_CODES_UK index that had already been created. Note that this statement would fail if any of the rows in column ABBR contain duplicates at the time of the statement.

Constraints can also be removed using the ALTER command. The following statement drops the primary key of the AIRPORTS table.

```
ALTER TABLE airports
DROP PRIMARY KEY CASCADE;

table AIRPORTS altered.
```

DROP

The DROP command is used to remove objects from the database. Unlike the CREATE and ALTER commands, DROP generally has very few options associated with it. Most often it simply consists of the DROP command followed by an object type and object name:

```
DROP object_type object_name;
```

As with the ALTER command, it can only act on objects that already exist. It is also important to note that while it is often possible to issue ROLLBACK commands to reverse DML operations, not all database platforms have a similar capability to reverse DDL operations. Once an object has been dropped, it may well be gone forever. Be wary when issuing DDL commands.

```
DROP VIEW aircraft_fleet_v;

view AIRCRAFT_FLEET_V dropped.
```

4.3 Form commands using Data Manipulation Language (DML)

Using the INSERT statement

You can add new rows to a table with the INSERT statement. The syntax of a single table INSERT is:

```
INSERT INTO table_name [(column [,column…])]
VALUES (value [, value…]);
```

In this statement, table_name is the table into which rows will be inserted, column is the name of the column(s) of the table values are being added to, and value is the data that will be inserted into the column. The column list is optional, but if omitted, the values clause must include all columns of the table in the order that they are recorded in the Oracle data dictionary. A column list allows you to insert into a subset of the table columns and explicitly match the order of the columns to the order of the values list. When writing SQL that will be reused, it is best practice to always explicitly list the columns in an insert statement. This makes the resulting code more robust if columns are added to the table at a later date. When there are multiple rows or columns, they are enclosed by parentheses and separated by commas.

The simplest form of an insert statement inserts a single row into a single table. The following inserts a new person into the EMPLOYEES table (described below).

```
desc employees
Name           Null     Type
-------------- -------- ------------
EMP_ID         NOT NULL NUMBER
AFL_ID                  NUMBER
EMP_FIRST               VARCHAR2(10)
EMP_LAST       NOT NULL VARCHAR2(10)
EMP_JOB                 VARCHAR2(10)
EMP_SUPERVISOR          NUMBER
SALARY                  NUMBER
START_DATE              DATE
```

```
INSERT INTO employees (emp_id, afl_id, emp_first,
                       emp_last, emp_job,
                       emp_supervisor, salary,
                       start_date)
VALUES (18, NULL, 'Guy', 'Newberry', 'Mgr', 8,
        98250, '07-JAN-2012');
```

Note that character data is enclosed by quotes as is the one date field. Numeric values being inserted into a NUMBER column are not generally enclosed by quotes, but it will not generate an error if you do (Oracle will implicitly convert the value back to a number data type during the INSERT operation). The NULL keyword cannot be enclosed in quotes. If the text NULL was enclosed in quotes, instead of a NULL value being inserted, the text 'NULL' would be inserted (or an error generated if the column were not a character field)..

The above INSERT statement contains all of the values of the EMPLOYEES table and the column order matches that in the data dictionary. The column list is therefore optional and the INSERT could have been written like this:

```
INSERT INTO employees
VALUES (18, NULL, 'Guy', 'Newberry', 'Mgr', 8,
        98250, '07-JAN-2012');
```

To insert into only a subset of columns in a table, you <u>must</u> provide a list of the columns that you wish to provide values for. Any columns not provided in the column list will contain a NULL after the INSERT operation unless they have a default value or are populated by a trigger. The following statement would insert a row into the employees table, leaving the SALARY and START_DATE fields NULL. Note that if either of the columns had a NOT NULL constraint, then the statement would fail.

```
INSERT INTO employees (emp_id, afl_id, emp_first, emp_last,
                       emp_job, emp_supervisor)
VALUES (18, NULL, 'Guy', 'Newberry', 'Mgr', 8);
```

The same operation could have been performed without a column list by explicitly adding the NULL values to the INSERT statement:

```
INSERT INTO employees
VALUES (18, NULL, 'Guy', 'Newberry', 'Mgr', 8, NULL, NULL);
```

Using the UPDATE statement

An UPDATE operation is used to modify existing data in a table. You can update a single row in a table, multiple rows using a filter, or the entire table. If an update does not contain a WHERE clause, every single row in the target table will be updated. The syntax for an UPDATE is:

```
UPDATE table_name
SET    column1 = value1 [, column2 = value2, ...]
[WHERE condition];
```

The following statement moves all of the employees that used to report to the employees with emp_id 9 to the new employee with emp_id 18. If no WHERE clause were supplied, all rows in the employees table would have the emp_supervisor field set to 18.

```
UPDATE employees
SET    emp_supervisor = 18
WHERE  emp_supervisor = 9;
```

The EMP_LAST column of the EMPLOYEES table has a NOT NULL constraint. Trying to set this field to NULL will generate an error:

```
UPDATE employees
SET    emp_last = NULL
WHERE  emp_id = 12;

SQL Error: ORA-01407: cannot update
("OCPGURU"."EMPLOYEES"."EMP_LAST") to NULL
01407. 00000 -  "cannot update (%s) to NULL"
```

As with the INSERT statement, it's possible to use a subquery to provide the data used for an UPDATE operation. The column count and order must match between the UPDATE and the results generated by the subquery. The syntax for this is:

```
UPDATE table_name
SET    (column1 [, column2 ...] = (SELECT column1 [, column2 ...] FROM
sqtab)
[WHERE condition];
```

Using the DELETE statement

The DELETE operation removes rows that already exist in a table. The syntax for a DELETE statement is:

```
DELETE
[FROM]  table_name
[WHERE  condition];
```

Only the keyword DELETE and a table name are required. If you issue the command 'DELETE employees', then all rows in the EMPLOYEES table will be deleted. The FROM keyword is seldom left off of DELETE statements in practice, but it is strictly optional. The following statement deletes from the EMPLOYEES table the employee with emp_id 9.

```
DELETE
FROM   employees
WHERE  emp_id = 9;
```

There is no data to be supplied for a DELETE operation as there is with INSERT and UPDATE operations. However, it's possible to use a subquery in the WHERE clause to dynamically build the filter of rows to be deleted. The following query would remove any aircraft from the AIRCRAFT_TYPES table that did not currently exist in the fleet.

```
DELETE FROM aircraft_types
WHERE  act_name NOT IN
       (SELECT act_name
        FROM   aircraft_fleet_v);
```

Querying data using SELECT

Essentially all operations that pull data out of a table in a relational database have a SELECT command involved at some level. A top-level SELECT statement is also referred to as a query. If there is a second SELECT nested within the first, it is called a subquery.

When a SELECT statement retrieves information from the database, it can perform the following three types of work:

- **Selection** -- You can filter the SELECT statement to choose only the rows that you want to be returned. Without filtering, a query would return every single row in the table.
- **Projection** -- You can choose only the columns that you want to be returned by your query, or create new information through the use of expressions.
- **Joining** -- You can use the SQL JOIN operators to link two or more tables to allow you to return data that is stored in more than one table.

The following diagram illustrates a query performing both selection and projection:

```
SELECT act_seats
FROM   aircraft_flights
WHERE  act_name = 'Boeing 787';
```

Projection (column)

Selection (row)

ACT_ID	ACT_NAME	ACT_BODY_STYLE	ACT_DECKS	ACT_SEATS
1	Boeing 747	Wide	Double	416
2	Boeing 767	Wide	Single	350
3	Boeing 737	Narrow	Single	200
4	Boeing 757	Narrow	Single	240
5	Boeing 777	Wide	Single	407
6	Boeing 787	Wide	Single	296
7	Airbus A320	Narrow	Single	200
8	Airbus A380	Wide	Double	525

The syntax of a minimal SELECT statement in ANSI SQL is:

```
SELECT select_list
FROM   table_reference;
```

The four elements above (SELECT and FROM keywords and the select_list and table_reference clauses) exist in every SQL query issued to a relational database (or at least every one that completes without an error). The elements that make up the **select_list** might be columns, functions, literals, etc. The **table_reference** might be a table, remote table, external table, view, etc. Regardless of the specifics, they must be valid references and be present in the SELECT statement in order for it to execute successfully.

The most basic SELECT statement consists of the SELECT keyword, a list of one or more columns or expressions (the select_list noted aboce), the FROM keyword, and a table or view (the table_reference value shown above). When executed with only the SELECT and FROM keywords, the database will return all rows that currently exist in the table and the order that the rows will be returned in is indeterminate (which is to say the order is not only unpredictable but may change from one execution to the next).

```
SELECT apt_id, apt_name, apt_abbr
FROM   airports;

APT_ID APT_NAME                       APT_ABBR
------ ------------------------------ --------
     1 Orlando, FL                    MCO
     2 Atlanta, GA                    ATL
     3 Miami, FL                      MIA
     4 Jacksonville, FL               JAX
     5 Dallas/Fort Worth              DFW
```

If you wish to display all columns from a table, rather than entering each column into the SELECT clause, you can use the asterisk wildcard. The asterisk will return the complete set of columns from the table (or tables) listed in the FROM clause. If a query contains multiple tables, you can prefix the asterisk with a table name or table alias to return all columns from just one of the tables in the query.

When the asterisk is used in a SELECT, the columns to be returned by the SELECT operation are pulled directly from the data dictionary table that is used to store column information for user tables. The columns in the SELECT list will appear in the order that they are stored in that table and cannot be altered. The column headings returned by the operation will be the upper-case column names as stored in the data dictionary. There is no way to use the asterisk *and* supply column aliases or change the column order.

```
SELECT *
FROM   airports;

APT_ID APT_NAME                       APT_ABBR
------ ------------------------------ --------
     1 Orlando, FL                    MCO
     2 Atlanta, GA                    ATL
     3 Miami, FL                      MIA
     4 Jacksonville, FL               JAX
     5 Dallas/Fort Worth              DFW
```

In the below example, the query contains two tables joined together. The asterisk used in the SELECT list returns all columns from both tables. Both tables contain a column called APT_ID (which is how the two are joined) and so that column is returned once for each table.

```
SELECT *
FROM   airports apt
       INNER JOIN aircraft_fleet afl
       ON apt.apt_id = afl.apt_id;

APT_ID APT_NAME               APT_ABBR AFL_ID ACT_ID APT_ID
------ ---------------------- -------- ------ ------ ------
     1 Orlando, FL            MCO           1      2      1
     1 Orlando, FL            MCO           2      2      1
     2 Atlanta, GA            ATL           3      3      2
     2 Atlanta, GA            ATL           4      4      2
     3 Miami, FL              MIA           5      1      3
     3 Miami, FL              MIA           6      1      3
     5 Dallas/Fort Worth      DFW           7      1      5
     5 Dallas/Fort Worth      DFW           8      2      5
```

When the asterisk is prefixed with the AIRPORTS table alias, only the columns from that table are returned:

```
SELECT apt.*
FROM   airports apt
       INNER JOIN aircraft_fleet afl
       ON apt.apt_id = afl.apt_id;

APT_ID APT_NAME               APT_ABBR
------ ---------------------- --------
     1 Orlando, FL            MCO
     1 Orlando, FL            MCO
     2 Atlanta, GA            ATL
     2 Atlanta, GA            ATL
     3 Miami, FL              MIA
     3 Miami, FL              MIA
     5 Dallas/Fort Worth      DFW
     5 Dallas/Fort Worth      DFW
```

In order to return a subset of the columns in the two tables and control the order of display, it is necessary to supply the columns to be returned:

```
SELECT APT_ABBR, APT_NAME, ACT_ID
FROM   airports apt
       INNER JOIN aircraft_fleet afl
       ON apt.apt_id = afl.apt_id;

APT_ABBR APT_NAME                  ACT_ID
-------- ---------------------- ----------
MCO      Orlando, FL                     2
MCO      Orlando, FL                     2
ATL      Atlanta, GA                     3
ATL      Atlanta, GA                     4
MIA      Miami, FL                       1
MIA      Miami, FL                       1
DFW      Dallas/Fort Worth               1
DFW      Dallas/Fort Worth               2
```

Restricting data in DML operations

The WHERE clause of SQL statements allows you to create conditions that rows must meet in order to be affected by a given DML operation. The conditions in the clause may be extremely simple or mind-numbingly complex. If you omit the WHERE clause in a query, all rows of the table or tables in the query will be affected by the SQL operation. In the case of a SELECT, this means all rows would be returned by the query. In the case of a DELETE or UPDATE, all rows in the table would be deleted or modified respectively.

The most common comparison operators for a WHERE clause are:

- = -- Equal to
- < -- Less than
- > -- Greater than
- <= -- Less than or equal to
- >= -- Greater than or equal to
- <> -- Greater than or Less than
- !=, ^= -- Not equal to
- **IN(set)** – Value contained within the comma-separated set
- **BETWEEN val1 AND val2** – Between val1 and val2 (inclusive)

- **LIKE** – Matches a given pattern that can include wildcards
- **IS NULL** – Is a NULL value
- **IS NOT NULL** – Is a non-NULL value

The equality operator is almost assuredly the most common condition applied to filter the data being returned from a SQL query. In the example below the query will return only those rows of the AIRCRAFT_TYPES table where the ACT_DECKS is equal to the text 'Single'.

```
SELECT *
FROM   aircraft_types
WHERE  act_decks = 'Single';

ACT_ID ACT_NAME     ACT_BODY_STYLE ACT_DECKS  ACT_SEATS
------ ------------ -------------- ---------- ---------
     2 Boeing 767   Wide           Single           350
     3 Boeing 737   Narrow         Single           200
     4 Boeing 757   Narrow         Single           240
```

The results of the above query can be completely reversed by using the not-equals operator '!='. This operator (or the alternate 'not equal' operator '^=') is interchangeable with the Greater than/Less than operator '<>'.

```
SELECT *
FROM   aircraft_types
WHERE  act_decks != 'Single';

ACT_ID ACT_NAME     ACT_BODY_STYLE ACT_DECKS  ACT_SEATS
------ ------------ -------------- ---------- ---------
     1 Boeing 747   Wide           Double           416
```

The example below makes use of the less-than sign '<' for filtering the results:

```
SELECT *
FROM   aircraft_types
WHERE  act_seats < 416;

ACT_ID ACT_NAME     ACT_BODY_STYLE ACT_DECKS  ACT_SEATS
------ ------------ -------------- ---------- ---------
     2 Boeing 767   Wide           Single           350
     3 Boeing 737   Narrow         Single           200
     4 Boeing 757   Narrow         Single           240
```

The example below makes use of the IN operator for filtering the results:

```
SELECT *
FROM   aircraft_types
WHERE  act_name IN ('Boeing 737', 'Boeing 767');

ACT_ID ACT_NAME     ACT_BODY_STYLE ACT_DECKS  ACT_SEATS
------ ------------ -------------- ---------- ---------
     2 Boeing 767   Wide           Single           350
     3 Boeing 737   Narrow         Single           200
```

The example below makes use of the BETWEEN operator for filtering the results. Note that the BETWEEN is inclusive because the endpoints of 200 and 240 are included in the results. If the BETWEEN operator were NOT inclusive, the range would need to have been 199 -> 241.

```
SELECT *
FROM   aircraft_types
WHERE  act_seats BETWEEN 200
                     AND 240;

ACT_ID ACT_NAME     ACT_BODY_STYLE ACT_DECKS  ACT_SEATS
------ ------------ -------------- ---------- ---------
     3 Boeing 737   Narrow         Single           200
     4 Boeing 757   Narrow         Single           240
```

The example below shows pattern matching using the LIKE operator. The % wildcard looks for zero or more occurrences of any character or combination of characters, whereas the _ wildcard looks for a single indeterminate character. The condition below then will return any aircraft where the number '5' is the second-to-last character in the string.

```
SELECT *
FROM   aircraft_types
WHERE  act_name LIKE '%5_';

ACT_ID ACT_NAME     ACT_BODY_STYLE ACT_DECKS  ACT_SEATS
------ ------------ -------------- ---------- ---------
     4 Boeing 757   Narrow         Single           240
```

If columns are aliased in the SELECT clause, the alias names cannot be used to reference columns in the WHERE clause. When the SQL engine parses the SQL, the WHERE clause gets evaluated before the aliases are applied, so the engine does not recognize the alias.

```
SELECT ACT_NAME        AS NAME,
       ACT_BODY_STYLE AS STYLE,
       ACT_DECKS       AS DECKS,
       ACT_SEATS       AS SEATS
FROM   aircraft_types
WHERE  decks = 'Single';

SQL Error: ORA-00904: "DECKS": invalid identifier
00904. 00000 -  "%s: invalid identifier"
*Cause:
*Action:
```

The following example is able to make use of the 'DECKS' alias in the WHERE clause, however. This is because the aliased columns are inside of parenthesis and the WHERE clause is outside. Just as with the earlier discussion on operators, the SQL engine will evaluate SQL text inside of parenthesis prior to SQL outside of it. By the time the WHERE clause is evaluated, the aliases have already been applied to the columns.

```
SELECT NAME, STYLE, DECKS, SEATS
FROM
(
SELECT ACT_NAME        AS NAME,
       ACT_BODY_STYLE AS STYLE,
       ACT_DECKS       AS DECKS,
       ACT_SEATS       AS SEATS
FROM   aircraft_types
)
WHERE  decks = 'Single';

NAME         STYLE      DECKS      SEATS
------------ ---------- ---------- -----
Boeing 767   Wide       Single       350
Boeing 737   Narrow     Single       200
Boeing 757   Narrow     Single       240
```

Combining two or more conditions with Logical Operators

There are three logical operators that can be used in conjunction with operators in a WHERE clause to generate more complex (and specific) logic for identifying rows:

- **AND** – Evaluates to TRUE if the components on both sides are TRUE.
- **OR** -- Evaluates to TRUE if the component on either side are TRUE.
- **NOT** – Evaluates to TRUE if the identified component is FALSE

When two or more conditions in a WHERE clause are combined (or reversed) through the use of logical operators, results are returned by the query only when the complete clause evaluates to TRUE. The following two examples make use of two conditions each, the first combined with the 'AND' operator and the second with the 'OR' operator. In the first statement, both conditions have to evaluate to TRUE for a row to be returned. In the second, a row is returned if either condition evaluates to TRUE.

```
SELECT *
FROM   aircraft_types
WHERE  act_seats < 416
AND    act_body_style = 'Narrow';

ACT_ID ACT_NAME     ACT_BODY_STYLE ACT_DECKS  ACT_SEATS
------ ------------ -------------- ---------- ---------
     3 Boeing 737   Narrow         Single           200
     4 Boeing 757   Narrow         Single           240
```

```
SELECT *
FROM   aircraft_types
WHERE  act_seats < 220
OR     act_decks = 'Double';

ACT_ID ACT_NAME     ACT_BODY_STYLE ACT_DECKS  ACT_SEATS
------ ------------ -------------- ---------- ---------
     1 Boeing 747   Wide           Double           416
     3 Boeing 737   Narrow         Single           200
```

If a WHERE clause contains a combination of both 'AND' and 'OR' operators, it is very likely that the conditions must be combined within parentheses for the desired results to be achieved. In the below example, the first condition excludes planes with more than one deck (the 747). This is AND'ed with the second condition that filters out planes with a wide body style deck (excluding the 747 and 767). The final condition is OR'd in and provides an exception for planes with more than 200 seats.

The intent of the final condition is to include the 767 but exclude the 747 (the logic being to have one deck and either a narrow body or greater than 200 seats). However, the result of the query has all four aircraft types. The reason for this is that the OR operator has equal precedence with the AND operator. The clause as written will return planes with the following conditions:

- A single deck and not a wide body style
- Greater than 200 seats

```
SELECT *
FROM   aircraft_types
WHERE  act_decks = 'Single'
AND    act_body_style != 'Wide'
OR     act_seats > 200;

ACT_ID ACT_NAME     ACT_BODY_STYLE ACT_DECKS  ACT_SEATS
------ ------------ -------------- ---------- ---------
     1 Boeing 747   Wide           Double           416
     2 Boeing 767   Wide           Single           350
     3 Boeing 737   Narrow         Single           200
     4 Boeing 757   Narrow         Single           240
```

To return the 767 and not the 747, the second and third conditions must be evaluated together and then the result ANDed to the first condition. To do this, the conditions must be enclosed by parentheses to change the order of evaluation. The updated clause will return planes with the following conditions:

- A single deck.
- Greater than 200 seats and not a wide body style.

```
SELECT *
FROM   aircraft_types
WHERE  act_decks = 'Single'
AND    (    act_body_style != 'Wide'
        OR  act_seats > 200);

ACT_ID ACT_NAME     ACT_BODY_STYLE ACT_DECKS  ACT_SEATS
------ ------------ -------------- ---------- ---------
     2 Boeing 767   Wide           Single           350
     3 Boeing 737   Narrow         Single           200
     4 Boeing 757   Narrow         Single           240
```

Changing the order of the conditions in the SELECT statement would also have altered the results. The better option is the parentheses, however. Parentheses make it clear from the outset which conditions are intended to be evaluated together.

```
SELECT *
FROM   aircraft_types
WHERE  act_body_style != 'Wide'
OR     act_seats > 200
AND    act_decks = 'Single';

ACT_ID ACT_NAME     ACT_BODY_STYLE ACT_DECKS  ACT_SEATS
------ ------------ -------------- ---------- ---------
     2 Boeing 767   Wide           Single           350
     3 Boeing 737   Narrow         Single           200
     4 Boeing 757   Narrow         Single           240
```

The NOT logical operator simply reverses a given operator. The statement below has the condition 'WHERE NOT act_decks = 'Single'. This could just as easily be written 'WHERE act_decks != 'Single'. However, NOT is the only practical way to reverse the BETWEEN, IN, IS NULL, or LIKE operators.

```
SELECT *
FROM   aircraft_types
WHERE  NOT act_decks = 'Single';

ACT_ID ACT_NAME     ACT_BODY_STYLE ACT_DECKS  ACT_SEATS
------ ------------ -------------- ---------- ---------
     1 Boeing 747   Wide           Double           416
```

Just as with the English language, double-negatives are possible. They should be avoided because they make the intent of the SQL harder to determine. The following statement returns rows where the number of decks is NOT not-equal to 'Single'. A query where the decks were equal to 'Single' would be much easier to read.

```
SELECT *
FROM   aircraft_types
WHERE  NOT act_decks != 'Single';

ACT_ID ACT_NAME     ACT_BODY_STYLE ACT_DECKS  ACT_SEATS
------ ------------ -------------- ---------- ---------
     2 Boeing 767   Wide           Single           350
     3 Boeing 737   Narrow         Single           200
     4 Boeing 757   Narrow         Single           240
```

Precedence in WHERE clauses

When evaluating a WHERE clause, the order in which Oracle executes each of the conditions and operations is of critical importance in what the final result will be. The rules of precedence according to the Oracle SQL Reference manual are:

1. Arithmetic Operators (+, - , *, /)
2. Concatenation Operator (||)
3. Comparison conditions (=, !=, <, >, <=, >=)
4. IS [NOT] NULL, LIKE, [NOT] BETWEEN, [NOT] IN, EXISTS, IS OF type
5. NOT logical condition
6. AND logical condition
7. OR logical condition

Note that other relational database my use a different order of precedence. You can override the default order of precedence by making use of parenthesis. When you have a particularly complex clause, adding parenthesis is often advisable even if not strictly required in order to make the order of precedence more evident.

Sorting data returned by a query

The ORDER BY clause of a SQL query allows you to determine the sort order of the rows returned by the operation. When a SQL statement does not contain an ORDER BY clause, the order of the rows being returned is indeterminate. Often rows will be returned in the order they were inserted into a table, but that is not always the case. The same query may not ever return rows in the same order in all cases. If the order is important, then you should use the ORDER BY clause even if you find that the rows return in the order you want without the clause (because the order might change at some future date). When the ORDER BY clause is used, it must always be the last clause of the SQL statement. When a SQL statement has subqueries, it is possible to use an ORDER BY clause for them, but generally pointless. The final ORDER BY determines the sort order of the data returned to the user. It is not possible to use LONG or LOB columns in an ORDER BY clause.

```
SELECT NAME, STYLE, DECKS, SEATS
FROM
(
SELECT ACT_NAME       AS NAME,
       ACT_BODY_STYLE AS STYLE,
       ACT_DECKS      AS DECKS,
       ACT_SEATS      AS SEATS
FROM   aircraft_types
ORDER BY act_seats
)
WHERE  decks = 'Single'
ORDER BY name;

NAME         STYLE      DECKS      SEATS
------------ ---------- ---------- -----
Boeing 737   Narrow     Single       200
Boeing 757   Narrow     Single       240
Boeing 767   Wide       Single       350
```

It's possible to sort by a single column or by multiple columns (or expressions). When sorting by multiple columns, the precedence of the sort order will be determined by the position of the expression in the ORDER BY clause. The leftmost expression will provide the initial sort order and each expression to the right will be evaluated in turn. By default, data is sorted in ascending order (1-2-3-4 / a-b-c-d). One item of note is the fact that upper and lower case characters don't sort together. When the Oracle database sorts by character values, it is actually using the ASCII values for the logic. Because of this, a lower case 'a' will sort *higher* than an upper case 'Z'. In addition, numeric data in a character field does not sort as you would expect. For example, if you were to sort table rows with values containing '1', '2', and '100' in ascending order, the result would be 1-100-2. To sort number data in a character field in numeric order, you would have to use the TO_NUMBER function against the column in the ORDER BY clause to convert the data for sort purposes. That said, if the column contains non-numeric data in addition to the numeric data, using TO_NUMBER will generate an error if it hits one of those rows.

```
SELECT char_column
FROM   sort_example
ORDER BY char_column;

CHAR_COLUMN
-----------
1
100
2
A
B
C
a
b
c
```

The SORT_EXAMPLE table has a NUMBER column as well. When a query is sorted by it, the expected 'numeric' sort results are returned.

```
SELECT num_column
FROM   sort_example
ORDER BY num_column;

NUM_COLUMN
----------
         1
         2
         3
        10
        20
        30
       100
       200
       300
```

If the data is sorted by the column after being converted to character data, the result is completely different:

```
SELECT num_column
FROM   sort_example
ORDER BY TO_CHAR(num_column);

NUM_COLUMN
----------
         1
        10
       100
         2
        20
       200
         3
        30
       300
```

By default NULLS are sorted last when a sort is in ascending order and first when descending. Effectively when being sorted, NULLs are treated as an infinitely high value. The default behavior can be reversed by adding NULLS LAST when sorting in descending order or NULLS FIRST when sorting in ascending order.

```
SELECT *
FROM   aircraft_fleet
ORDER BY apt_id;

AFL_ID ACT_ID APT_ID
------ ------ ------
     1      2      1
     2      2      1
     3      3      2
     4      4      2
     5      1      3
     6      1      3
     7      1      5
     8      2      5
     9      4
    10      3
```

```
SELECT *
FROM   aircraft_fleet
ORDER BY apt_id NULLS FIRST;

AFL_ID ACT_ID APT_ID
------ ------ ------
     9      4
    10      3
     2      2      1
     1      2      1
     3      3      2
     4      4      2
     6      1      3
     5      1      3
     7      1      5
     8      2      5
```

When specifying the expressions to sort by, you can use either the expression itself, the alias for the expression, or the numeric value of its position in the SELECT list. Using the position rather than the expression can be useful of the expression being sorted on is complex. It is also useful when sorting compound queries using the set operators (UNION, INTERSECT, MINUS) where the column names may not match. Set operators will be discussed in a later section.

```
SELECT APT_ID, APT_NAME, APT_ABBR
FROM   airports
ORDER BY apt_name;

APT_ID APT_NAME                         APT_ABBR
------ -------------------------------- --------
     2 Atlanta, GA                      ATL
     5 Dallas/Fort Worth                DFW
     4 Jacksonville, FL                 JAX
     3 Miami, FL                        MIA
     1 Orlando, FL                      MCO
```

```
SELECT *
FROM   airports
ORDER BY 2;

APT_ID APT_NAME                         APT_ABBR
------ -------------------------------- --------
     2 Atlanta, GA                      ATL
     5 Dallas/Fort Worth                DFW
     4 Jacksonville, FL                 JAX
     3 Miami, FL                        MIA
     1 Orlando, FL                      MCO
```

To reverse the sort order of columns, you can use the descending operator, DESC.

```
SELECT *
FROM   airports
ORDER BY 2 DESC;

APT_ID APT_NAME                 APT_ABBR
------ ------------------------ --------
     1 Orlando, FL              MCO
     3 Miami, FL                MIA
     4 Jacksonville, FL         JAX
     5 Dallas/Fort Worth        DFW
     2 Atlanta, GA              ATL
```

The default sort order on columns is always ascending. If a column is sorted on more than one column, and you want to change multiple columns to sort in descending order, each would need its own DESC keyword. The following query sorts by three columns. First it sorts all the rows by the EMP_JOB field in ascending order. For all employees in the same job, it sorts rows by the AIRCRAFT_TYPE in descending order. For all rows with the same job and aircraft type, it sorts in ascending order by last name.

```
SELECT emp_job,
        (SELECT act_name
         FROM   aircraft_types act
                NATURAL JOIN aircraft_fleet afl
         WHERE  afl.afl_id = e1.afl_id) AS aircraft_type,
        emp_last,
       (SELECT emp_last
        FROM employees e2
        WHERE e2.emp_id = e1.emp_supervisor) AS MANAGER
FROM   employees e1
ORDER BY emp_job, aircraft_type DESC, emp_last;

EMP_JOB    AIRCRAFT_TYPE EMP_LAST   MANAGER
---------- ------------- ---------- ----------
CEO                      Boss
CFO                      Smith      Boss
Mgr                      Storm      Alien
Pilot      Boeing 767    Gun        Storm
Pilot      Boeing 767    Jones      Storm
Pilot      Boeing 767    Kia        Storm
Pilot      Boeing 757    Thomas     Storm
Pilot      Boeing 747    Aptop      Storm
Pilot      Boeing 747    Picard     Storm
Pilot      Boeing 747    Skytalker  Storm
Pilot      Boeing 737    McCoy      Storm
SVP                      Jameson    Boss
SVP                      Stoner     Boss
SrDir                    Alien      Jeckson
SrDir                    Stoneflint Abong
VP                       Abong      Jameson
VP                       Jeckson    Stoner
```

Unlike the WHERE clause, aliases can be used in the ORDER BY clause. The reason for this is because the SQL engine evaluates the WHERE clause before the select list but the ORDER BY clause after the select list.

```
SELECT APT_ID,
       APT_NAME AS AIRPORT_NAME,
       APT_ABBR AS ABBREV
FROM   airports
ORDER BY airport_name;

APT_ID AIRPORT_NAME            ABBREV
------ ----------------------- ------
     2 Atlanta, GA             ATL
     5 Dallas/Fort Worth       DFW
     4 Jacksonville, FL        JAX
     3 Miami, FL               MIA
     1 Orlando, FL             MCO
```

4.4 Use Data Control Language (DCL) statements to control the access to data in a database and to grant users permissions for data operations

Data control language

Depending on the RDBMS, there are only two or three commands in the Data Control Language. All relational databases (that I am aware of) have the GRANT and REVOKE commands. Some vendors also have a third command called DENY.

GRANT

In order to access tables that are owned by another schema, you must have been granted access to do so. This might be through a system privilege such as SELECT ANY TABLE, or by a grant on the table itself by the schema owner, or a schema that has privileges that allow it to grant the required access. Until a privilege has been granted, a RDBMS will treat attempts to SELECT from it as if the table does not even exist.

```
SELECT *
FROM   hr.regions;

ORA-00942: table or view does not exist
00942. 00000 -  "table or view does not exist"
*Cause:
*Action:
```

The basic syntax of the GRANT COMMAND is as follows:

```
GRANT [privilege]
ON [object]
TO [user]
[WITH GRANT OPTION]
```

The GRANT command is used to grant specific privileges to a user. In the following example, the SELECT privilege is granted to the querying schema. After the grant has completed, the above statement will succeed:

```
GRANT SELECT ON hr.regions TO ocpguru;

GRANT succeeded.

SELECT *
FROM   hr.regions;

REGION_ID REGION_NAME
--------- -------------------------
        1 Europe
        2 Americas
        3 Asia
        4 Middle East and Africa
```

There are a number of different privileges beyond SELECT that can be granted to a user. These can be granted as object privileges where they are applicable only for a specific object in the data dictionary or as a system privilege where they cover all objects. Some of these include:

- **DELETE** -- Delete rows in a table.
- **INSERT** -- Insert rows in a table.
- **UPDATE** -- Update data in a table or a subset of columns in a table.
- **REFERENCES** -- Create a foreign key reference on a table or a subset of columns in a table.
- **TRIGGER** -- Create a trigger on a table or a subset of columns in a table.

It is possible to grant multiple privileges in a single statement by providing a comma-separated list. It is also possible to grant one or more privileges to multiple users in the same fashion. The following example grants the UPDATE and DELETE privileges to the users JJONES and NGREENBE:

```
GRANT update, delete ON aircraft_types TO jjones, ngreenbe;
GRANT succeeded.
```

REVOKE

To remove a privilege that has been granted, the REVOKE statement is required. The syntax for the REVOKE command is defined as follows:

```
REVOKE [GRANT OPTION FOR] [permission]
ON [object]
FROM [user];
```

For example:

```
REVOKE SELECT ON hr.regions FROM ocpguru;

REVOKE succeeded.
```

It is also possible to revoke multiple privileges, or all privileges against an object in a single statement:

```
REVOKE ALL ON hr.regions FROM ocpguru;

REVOKE succeeded.
```

DENY

The DENY command is available in some relational databases. It can be used to explicitly prevent a user from receiving a particular permission. This might be applicable when the user is a member of a role or group that has been granted a large set of permissions. Most of the privileges included in the role are acceptable, but you want them to be excepted from one or more permissions contained within it. The syntax for the DENY command is as follows:

```
DENY [permission]
ON [object]
TO [user]
```

For example, if you wished to ensure that the OCPREP user would never receive the ability to delete information from the employees table, you would issue the following command:

```
DENY DELETE
ON HR.employees
TO ocprep;
```

Domain 5: Relational Algebra and Databases

5.1 Define and describe the use of relational algebra in order to create new relationships from existing database relations

Introduction to relational algebra

Relational algebra is a procedural query language that is the basis for the query capabilities of the SQL language. It is comprised of a set of algebraic operators that take one or two relations as input and produce a new relation as their result. As noted earlier in the guide, when working in relational algebra, relations equates to tables and tuples are equivalent to rows. After making that mental conversion -- the operations of relational algebra mirrors what would happen in the SQL operations that were derived from relational algebra. The operations possible in relational algebra include the following:

- **Assignment** -- Used to assign expressions to a temporary relation variable.
- **Cartesian Product** -- Allows for combination of information from any two relations.
- **Division** -- Used in queries wanting to find results including the phrase "for all".
- **Project** -- Used to return an argument with certain attributes left out.
- **Rename** -- Allows the results of a relational-algebra expression to be assigned a name, which can later be used to refer to them.
- **Select** -- Allows the selection of tuples that satisfy a given predicate.
- **Set Difference** -- Allows for finding tuples that are in one relation but are not in another.
- **Set Intersection** -- Results in the tuples that are in both relations the operation is applying to.
- **Union** -- Yields the relation of all tuples shared by two relations.

Each of the above has a symbol used to indicate the operation being performed when it is used in a relational algebra equation. Those symbols are shown in the figure below:

← Assignment
X Cartesian Product
÷ Division
Π Project
ρ Rename
Σ Select
- Set Difference
∩ Set Intersection
U Union

There are six operations in relational algebra that are considered fundamental. It is possible to define any retrieval using these six operators alone.

- Select
- Project
- Rename
- Union
- Set Difference
- Cartesian Product

There are several additional operators that are convenient, but are not fundamental operations. Using these operators can simplify the process of retrieving a desired result, but they are not required. Any operation that can be performed by the below set could be performed by some combination of the fundamental operations.

- Set Intersection
- Natural Join
- Division
- Assignment

Operations can either be unary or binary. Unary operations take a single relation as an operand. Binary operations require two relations as an operand. Regardless of whether an operation takes one or two relations as operands, it returns a single relation as a result. It is possible to nest multiple operations within each other.

Predicates are BOOLEAN expressions that refer to attributes in a relation (r) and compares them either to constant values or other attributes. Some of the predicates include:

- = -- Equal to
- ≠ -- Not equal to
- < -- Less than
- > -- Greater than
- <= -- Less than or equal to
- >= -- Greater than or equal to

Selection

By definition, a relational database is a set of relations r, each of which belongs to a particular relation schema R. The select operation is a unary operation on a given relation r that is denoted by the lowercase Greek letter sigma (σ) and includes a predicate p. This operation allows you to select only the tuples that satisfy a given predicate. It is written as:

$$\sigma p(r)$$

The AIRPORTS table is shown below:

AIRPORTS

APT_ID	APT_NAME	APT_ABBR
1	Orlando, FL	MCO
2	Atlanta, GA	ATL
3	Miami, FL	MIA
4	Jacksonville, FL	JAX
5	Dallas/Fort Worth	DFW
7	Houston, TX	IAH

The following select operation would return the tuples of the AIRPORTS relation where the airport abbreviation is "IAH":

$\sigma_{\text{APT\_ABBR = "IAH"}}$ (AIRPORTS)

The result of the operation would be a relation with a single tuple:

AIRPORTS

APT_ID	APT_NAME	APT_ABBR
7	Houston, TX	IAH

It is also possible to use other predicates such as < or >. An example query against the AIRCRAFT_TYPES relation uses the 'greater than' predicate to find all tuples in which the ACT_SEATS value is greater than 400 is shown below:

AIRCRAFT TYPES

ACT_ID	ACT_NAME	ACT_BODY	ACT_DECKS	ACT_SEATS
1	Boeing 747	Wide	Double	416
2	Boeing 767	Wide	Single	350
3	Boeing 737	Narrow	Single	200
4	Boeing 757	Narrow	Single	240
5	Boeing 777	Wide	Single	407
6	Boeing 787	Wide	Single	296

$\sigma_{\text{ACT\_SEATS > 400}}$ (AIRCRAFT_TYPES)

The result of the operation would be the following relation with two tuples:

AIRCRAFT TYPES

ACT_ID	ACT_NAME	ACT_BODY	ACT_DECKS	ACT_SEATS
1	Boeing 747	Wide	Double	416
5	Boeing 777	Wide	Single	407

It is possible for multiple predicates can be combined into larger predicates using connectives:

- **^** -- The AND connective evaluates to TRUE if the predicates on both sides are TRUE.
- **V** -- The OR connective evaluates to TRUE if the predicates on either side is TRUE.

An example using a connective is to find those tuples pertaining to aircraft with more than 300 seats and a single deck is written as:

$\sigma_{ACT\_SEATS > 300 \wedge ACT\_DECKS = \text{"Single"}}(AIRCRAFT\_TYPES)$

The result of the operation would be the following relation with two tuples:

AIRCRAFT TYPES

ACT_ID	ACT_NAME	ACT_BODY	ACT_DECKS	ACT_SEATS
2	Boeing 767	Wide	Single	350
5	Boeing 777	Wide	Single	407

Projection

The projection operation is a unary operation on a relation r that is denoted by uppercase Greek letter pi (Π) and includes an attribute list A. It is written as:

$$\Pi_A(r)$$

It returns its argument relation with certain attributes left out. Because a relation is a set, any duplicate tuples in the result are eliminated. In the example below, the query to list all aircraft names and the number of seats is written as:

$$\Pi_{ACT\_NAME,ACT\_SEATS}(AIRCRAFT\_TYPES)$$

The result of the operation would be the following:

AIRCRAFT TYPES

ACT_NAME	ACT_SEATS
Boeing 747	416
Boeing 767	350
Boeing 737	200
Boeing 757	240
Boeing 777	407
Boeing 787	296

A more complicated example below combines projection with selection to return only the names of aircraft with less than 300 seats:

$$\Pi_{ACT\_NAME}(\sigma_{ACT\_SEATS < 300}(AIRCRAFT\_TYPES))$$

AIRCRAFT TYPES

ACT_NAME
Boeing 737
Boeing 757
Boeing 787

Cartesian product

The Cartesian-product operation is a binary operation on relations r1 and r2 that is denoted by X. It is written as:

r1 X r2

The result of a Cartesian operation is that every tuple in relation r1 is joined with every tuple in relation r2. The result is a relation with a number of tuples equal to the count from r1 times the count from r2. The example Cartesian operation below uses the AIRPORTS and AIRCRAFT_TYPES tables as the relations.

AIRPORTS X AIRCRAFT_TYPES

Since each of them has six tuples, the resulting relation contains thirty-six tuples. To save space, the image below shows only a portion of the result of the above operation:

APT_ID	APT_NAME	APT_ABBR	ACT_ID	ACT_NAME	ACT_BODY_STYLE	ACT_DECKS	ACT_SEATS
1	Orlando, FL	MCO	1	Boeing 747	Wide	Double	416
2	Atlanta, GA	ATL	1	Boeing 747	Wide	Double	416
3	Miami, FL	MIA	1	Boeing 747	Wide	Double	416
4	Jacksonville, FL	JAX	1	Boeing 747	Wide	Double	416
5	Dallas/Fort Worth	DFW	1	Boeing 747	Wide	Double	416
7	Houston, TX	IAH	1	Boeing 747	Wide	Double	416
1	Orlando, FL	MCO	2	Boeing 767	Wide	Single	350
2	Atlanta, GA	ATL	2	Boeing 767	Wide	Single	350
3	Miami, FL	MIA	2	Boeing 767	Wide	Single	350
4	Jacksonville, FL	JAX	2	Boeing 767	Wide	Single	350
...	...	...	...	...	...	...	...
4	Jacksonville, FL	JAX	6	Boeing 787	Wide	Single	296
5	Dallas/Fort Worth	DFW	6	Boeing 787	Wide	Single	296
7	Houston, TX	IAH	6	Boeing 787	Wide	Single	296

The raw result of a cartesian product is not particularly useful. In practice, when the cartesian operation is used in relational algebra, a select operation is performed on the Cartesian product as part of the equation. The select condition is designed to return a meaningful connection between some attribute(s) of r1 and r2. In terms of actual SQL operations in the real world, cartesian products generally only happen by accident. There is essentially no reason to use them.

Union

The union operation is a binary operation on relations r and s that is denoted by the symbol U. It is written as:

$$r \cup s$$

The union operation yields the distinct results that appear in either or both of two relations. None of the Imaginary Airlines tables are good candidates for a union operation, so the tables below, TABLE_SETA and TABLE_SETB will be used. A query that unions the results between COL1 of the two tables would be written:

TABLE_SETA

COL1
A
A
A
A
B
C

TABLE_SETB

COL1
B
B
C
C
D
D
D

$$\sigma_{COL1}(TABLE\_SETA) \cup \sigma_{COL1}(TABLE\_SETB)$$

The results of the operation would be the following:

COL1
A
B
C
D

For a union operation r U s to be valid, two conditions must be true:

1. The relation r and s must be of the same arity. That is, they must have the same number of attributes.
2. The domains of the attribute i of r and the attribute i of s must be the same, for all i. For example, if the first attribute of r is numeric, the first attribute of s must also be numeric.

Difference

The set-difference operation is a binary operation on relations r and s that is denoted by the symbol –. It is written as:

$$r - s$$

The result is a new relation consisting of tuples t such that t is contained within r but t is not contained within s. Once again, the tables TABLE_SETA and TABLE_SETB will be used for the example. A query that returns the difference of the COL1 values in the two tables would be written:

TABLE_SETA

COL1
A
A
A
A
B
C

TABLE_SETB

COL1
B
B
C
C
D
D
D

$$\sigma_{COL1}(TABLE\_SETA) - \sigma_{COL1}(TABLE\_SETB)$$

The results of the operation would be the following:

COL1
A

As with a union operation a set-difference operation is only valid for compatible relations. They must have the same arity and corresponding domains.

Intersection

The intersect operation is a binary operation on relations r and s that is denoted by the symbol ∩. It is written as:

$r \cap s$

The set intersection is not a fundamental operation. However, it is a more convenient way to write r - (r - s). The result is a new relation consisting of tuples t such that t is contained within r and t is also contained within s. The tables TABLE_SETA and TABLE_SETB will be used for the example. A query that returns the intersect of the COL1 values in the two tables would be written:

$$\sigma_{COL1}(TABLE\_SETA) \cap \sigma_{COL1}(TABLE\_SETB)$$

The results of the operation would be the following:

COL1
B
C

As with a union operation an intersect operation is only valid for compatible relations. They must have the same arity and corresponding domains.

5.2 Compose joins in a database

Joins

Any query that combines rows from two or more tables, views, materialized views, subqueries, or table functions must make use of joins (henceforth I'll use the word 'table' to mean any of these). Relational databases must perform a join operation any time multiple tables appear in the FROM clause of the query.

There are a number of different join types possible, including:

- **EQUIJOIN** -- A join where the condition contains an equality operator. An equijoin combines rows that have equivalent values for the specified columns.
- **NON-EQUIJOIN** -- A join where the condition does not contain an equality operator – (e.g. the operator might be greater than or less than). A non-equijoin combines rows that have non-equivalent values for the specified columns.
- **SELF-JOIN** -- A join of a table back to itself. The given table will appear twice (or more) in the FROM clause. All incarnations should have table aliases to allow you to qualify column names in the join condition and other parts of the query.
- **INNER JOIN** -- An inner join (sometimes called a simple join) is a join of two or more tables that returns only those rows that satisfy the join condition.
- **FULL OUTER JOIN** -- An outer join returns all rows that satisfy the join condition and also returns all of those rows from the tables for which no rows from the other satisfy the join condition.
- **LEFT OUTER JOIN –** A left join is a subset of the outer join where all of the rows in the table on the left-side in the FROM clause are returned and only the rows that meet the join condition are returned from the table on the right side in the FROM clause.
- **RIGHT OUTER JOIN –** A right join is the opposite of the left join. All of the rows in the table identified on the right-side in the FROM clause are returned and only the rows that meet the join condition are returned from the table on the left side in the FROM clause.
- **CROSS JOIN --** A cross join is the result when two tables are included in a query but no join condition is specified. When this is the case, Oracle returns the Cartesian product of the two tables (this is sometimes called a Cartesian Join). The Cartesian product is when every row of one table is joined with every row of the other. Generally considered to be useless, cross joins are most often created by mistake.

- **NATURAL JOIN** – A natural join can only be used when the column names and data types used for the join match in both tables. It will perform an inner-equijoin between the two tables.

Note that the above definitions are not exclusive. A join will often fulfill more than one of these definitions at a time. For example, a natural join is always an equijoin and an inner join. A self join is probably an equijoin an inner join as well.

When multiple tables exist in the FROM clause, the select list can include any combination of columns from any of the tables. When more than one table has a column name in common, then references to duplicated columns must be qualified in all parts of the query (with the exception of join columns in NATURAL or JOIN USING joins). A column name is qualified by prefixing it with the table name followed by a period, or with the table alias followed by a period.

The following example joins three tables together: AIRPORTS, AIRCRAFT_FLEET and AIRCRAFT_TYPES. A given join always involves only two database objects (with said object coming from the list mentioned in the previous section: tables, views, materialized views, subqueries, or table functions). It is not possible to join three or more objects together with a single join.

Connecting the three tables therefore requires two join operations. First AIRPORTS is joined to the AIRCRAFT_FLEET table using the APT_ID column that exists in both tables. Second, the AIRCRAFT_FLEET table is joined to the AIRCRAFT_TYPES table by the ACT_ID column that exists in both tables. The AIRPORTS and AIRCRAFT_TYPES tables are not directly joined in the SQL statement. The connection between these two tables is made through the AIRCRAFT_FLEET table that both are joined to.

```
SELECT apt_name, apt_abbr, act_name, act_seats
FROM   airports apt
       INNER JOIN aircraft_fleet afl
       ON apt.apt_id = afl.apt_id
       INNER JOIN aircraft_types act
       ON act.act_id = afl.act_id;

APT_NAME             APT_ABBR ACT_NAME     ACT_SEATS
-------------------- -------- ------------ ---------
Orlando, FL          MCO      Boeing 767         350
Orlando, FL          MCO      Boeing 767         350
Atlanta, GA          ATL      Boeing 757         240
Atlanta, GA          ATL      Boeing 737         200
Miami, FL            MIA      Boeing 747         416
Miami, FL            MIA      Boeing 747         416
Dallas/Fort Worth    DFW      Boeing 767         350
Dallas/Fort Worth    DFW      Boeing 747         416
```

Any SQL on the exam will conform to the ANSI SQL model. ANSI SQL is an industry standard and learning it as opposed to more proprietary versions makes your skills more marketable. If your career working with databases is long enough, you are likely to work with SQL from more than one vendor. I would recommend that you make use of ANSI SQL for that reason alone. The syntax for a join operation using ANSI SQL:1999 syntax is:

```
SELECT t1.*, t2.*
FROM   table1 t1
       [NATURAL JOIN table2 t2] |
       [JOIN table2 t2 USING (col_name)] |
       [INNER JOIN table2 t2
        ON (t1.col1 = t2.col2)] |
       [LEFT|RIGHT|FULL OUTER JOIN table2 t2
        ON (t1.col1 = t2.col2)] |
       [CROSS JOIN table2 t2];
```

Qualifying column names

When performing a SELECT operation against a single table, there is never any question of what table a given column name in the query belongs to. When multiple tables are joined together, however, it's possible for a query to reference a column name that exists in more than one of the joined tables. When this happens, the database must have a means of identifying the correct column. The method by which this is done is called qualifying the column. The table name or table alias is placed in front of the column name followed by a period (i.e. table_name.column_name or table_alias.column_name). It is not required to prefix columns where the table name can be determined by the SQL parser, but doing so makes the SQL more readable and provides a slight performance improvement during the parse operation.

When a table has been aliased in a query, it is not legal to use the table name as a prefix – you must use the alias. Using the table name will generate an error.

```
SELECT airports.apt_name, airports.apt_abbr
FROM   airports ap;

SQL Error: ORA-00904: "AIRPORTS"."APT_ABBR": invalid identifier
00904. 00000 -  "%s: invalid identifier"
*Cause:
*Action:
```

If the table is given no alias, then using the full name for a column prefix is legal (and the only way to qualify the column):

```
SELECT airports.apt_name, airports.apt_abbr
FROM   airports;

APT_NAME                APT_ABBR
----------------------- --------
Orlando, FL             MCO
Atlanta, GA             ATL
Miami, FL               MIA
Jacksonville, FL        JAX
Dallas/Fort Worth       DFW
```

If the table is given an alias, then you must use the alias as a column prefix or no prefix at all:

```
SELECT apt.apt_name, apt_abbr
FROM   airports apt;

APT_NAME               APT_ABBR
---------------------- --------
Orlando, FL            MCO
Atlanta, GA            ATL
Miami, FL              MIA
Jacksonville, FL       JAX
Dallas/Fort Worth      DFW
```

Equijoins

The vast majority of JOIN operations use equijoins. In an equijoin there is a condition such that column A in table one EQUALS column B in table two. As a general rule, when there's a need to join two tables, it will be by column data that is exactly equal. The below query uses three equijoins and connects four tables together to generate the required results.

```
SELECT apt_name, act_name, emp_first, emp_last
FROM   airports apt
       INNER JOIN aircraft_fleet afl
       ON apt.apt_id = afl.apt_id
       INNER JOIN aircraft_types act
       ON act.act_id = afl.act_id
       INNER JOIN employees emp
       ON afl.afl_id = emp.afl_id;

APT_NAME              ACT_NAME     EMP_FIRST   EMP_LAST
--------------------- ------------ ----------- --------------
Orlando, FL           Boeing 767   John        Jones
Orlando, FL           Boeing 767   Top         Gun
Atlanta, GA           Boeing 737   Phil        McCoy
Atlanta, GA           Boeing 757   James       Thomas
Miami, FL             Boeing 747   John        Picard
Miami, FL             Boeing 747   Luke        Skytalker
Dallas/Fort Worth     Boeing 747   Dell        Aptop
Dallas/Fort Worth     Boeing 767   Noh         Kia
```

Because the joins in the above example all are equijoins where the column names match in both tables, the NATURAL JOIN could have been used to generate the same result. If the join column(s) for a NATURAL JOIN are included anywhere else in the query, they should not be qualified with the table name or alias. Many SQL developers (myself included) prefer not to make use of the NATURAL JOIN syntax. When this type of join is used, the join column(s) being used to connect the two tables is not obvious without looking at the table structure. It is also possible to get unexpected results when join being made is not what the developer anticipated. Without looking at the SQL execution plan or performing detailed analysis of the rows returned, this can go unnoticed and generate erroneous data.

```
SELECT apt_name, act_name, emp_first, emp_last
FROM   airports apt
       NATURAL JOIN aircraft_fleet afl
       NATURAL JOIN aircraft_types act
       NATURAL JOIN employees emp;

APT_NAME             ACT_NAME     EMP_FIRST   EMP_LAST
-------------------- ------------ ----------- --------------
Orlando, FL          Boeing 767   John        Jones
Orlando, FL          Boeing 767   Top         Gun
Atlanta, GA          Boeing 737   Phil        McCoy
Atlanta, GA          Boeing 757   James       Thomas
Miami, FL            Boeing 747   John        Picard
Miami, FL            Boeing 747   Luke        Skytalker
Dallas/Fort Worth    Boeing 747   Dell        Aptop
Dallas/Fort Worth    Boeing 767   Noh         Kia
```

A third equivalent option for the query is the JOIN...USING syntax. When the USING clause is utilized, only the column name(s) for the JOIN get specified. JOIN..USING is a more flexible means of performing tables with identical column names than a NATURAL join. Just as with a NATURAL JOIN, it is always an EQUIJOIN and the join column names must always be the same in both tables. However, with JOIN...USING, the columns need not be the exact same data type (i.e. one could be CHAR and another VARCHAR or NCHAR). A NATURAL join between two tables will also join by all columns in the two tables that have matching names. The USING clause can specify a subset of columns with matching names. As with a NATURAL join, if the join column(s) are included anywhere else in the query, they should not be qualified with the table name or alias.

```
SELECT apt_name, act_name, emp_first, emp_last
FROM   airports apt
       JOIN aircraft_fleet afl USING (apt_id)
       JOIN aircraft_types act USING (act_id)
       JOIN employees emp USING (afl_id);
```

```
APT_NAME                    ACT_NAME       EMP_FIRST    EMP_LAST
--------------------- ------------ ----------- --------------
Orlando, FL                 Boeing 767     John         Jones
Orlando, FL                 Boeing 767     Top          Gun
Atlanta, GA                 Boeing 737     Phil         McCoy
Atlanta, GA                 Boeing 757     James        Thomas
Miami, FL                   Boeing 747     John         Picard
Miami, FL                   Boeing 747     Luke         Skytalker
Dallas/Fort Worth           Boeing 747     Dell         Aptop
Dallas/Fort Worth           Boeing 767     Noh          Kia
```

Finally a fourth syntax option for the query is the JOIN...ON syntax. This is nothing more than the 'INNER JOIN...ON' syntax with the optional 'INNER' left off. However, it's easy to confuse with the JOIN...USING syntax. When the ON syntax is used, the join condition must specify the join columns from both tables (qualified if they are the same name) and the operator. If the join columns are in the SELECT list, they must be qualified with a table name or alias.

```
SELECT apt_name, act_name, emp_first, emp_last
FROM   airports apt
       JOIN aircraft_fleet afl ON (apt.apt_id = afl.apt_id)
       JOIN aircraft_types act ON (afl.act_id = act.act_id)
       JOIN employees emp ON (afl.afl_id = emp.afl_id);
```

```
APT_NAME                    ACT_NAME       EMP_FIRST    EMP_LAST
---------------------- ------------ ---------- ----------
Orlando, FL                 Boeing 767     John         Jones
Orlando, FL                 Boeing 767     Top          Gun
Atlanta, GA                 Boeing 737     Phil         McCoy
Atlanta, GA                 Boeing 757     James        Thomas
Miami, FL                   Boeing 747     John         Picard
Miami, FL                   Boeing 747     Luke         Skytalker
Dallas/Fort Worth           Boeing 747     Dell         Aptop
Dallas/Fort Worth           Boeing 767     Noh          Kia
```

NonEquijoins

On occasion, there is a need to perform a non-equijoin. In a non-equijoin, the condition joining the columns of the two tables uses some condition other than EQUALS. In the below example, the EMPLOYEES table is joined to the SALARY_RANGES table. The join operation uses the BETWEEN operator to find which range each employee's salary falls into in order to determine the salary code.

```
SELECT emp.emp_first, emp.emp_last, salary, slr_code
FROM   employees emp
       INNER JOIN salary_ranges slr
       ON emp.salary BETWEEN slr.slr_lowval
                         AND slr.slr_highval
ORDER BY slr_code DESC;

EMP_FIRST    EMP_LAST          SALARY SLR_CODE
------------ ----------------- ------ --------
Big          Boss              197500 S09
Adam         Smith             157000 S07
Rob          Stoner            149100 S07
Rick         Jameson           145200 S07
Janet        Jeckson           127800 S06
Bill         Abong             123500 S06
Norm         Storm             101500 S05
Fred         Stoneflint        111500 S05
Alf          Alien             110500 S05
Luke         Skytalker          90000 S04
Dell         Aptop              87500 S04
Phil         McCoy              93500 S04
Noh          Kia                92250 S04
Top          Gun                91500 S04
John         Picard             94500 S04
James        Thomas             98500 S04
John         Jones              97500 S04
```

Additional JOIN conditions

You can add additional conditions to the JOIN clause when joining two tables together.

```
SELECT apt_name, act_name, emp_first, emp_last
FROM   airports apt
       JOIN aircraft_fleet afl ON (apt.apt_id = afl.apt_id)
       JOIN aircraft_types act ON (afl.act_id = act.act_id)
                              AND act.act_name='Boeing 767'
       JOIN employees emp ON (afl.afl_id = emp.afl_id);

APT_NAME                ACT_NAME     EMP_FIRST  EMP_LAST
----------------------- ------------ ---------- ----------
Orlando, FL             Boeing 767   John       Jones
Orlando, FL             Boeing 767   Top        Gun
Dallas/Fort Worth       Boeing 767   Noh        Kia
```

The result of adding this condition to the JOIN clause is indistinguishable from adding the same condition to the WHERE clause. Both will produce identical results.

```
SELECT apt_name, act_name, emp_first, emp_last
FROM   airports apt
       JOIN aircraft_fleet afl ON (apt.apt_id = afl.apt_id)
       JOIN aircraft_types act ON (afl.act_id = act.act_id)
       JOIN employees emp ON (afl.afl_id = emp.afl_id)
WHERE  act.act_name='Boeing 767';

APT_NAME                ACT_NAME     EMP_FIRST  EMP_LAST
----------------------- ------------ ---------- ----------
Orlando, FL             Boeing 767   John       Jones
Orlando, FL             Boeing 767   Top        Gun
Dallas/Fort Worth       Boeing 767   Noh        Kia
```

Self joins

It's sometimes useful to join a table back to itself when one column in it references data in a second column in the table. Earlier in this guide this was referred to as a recursive relationship (and potentially a hierarchical recursive relationship). In the example below, we join the EMPLOYEES table back to itself by using the EMP_ID and EMP_SUPERVISOR columns. In this fashion we're able to display each employee's immediate manager.

```
SELECT emp.emp_first, emp.emp_last, mgr.emp_first || ' ' ||
mgr.emp_last AS EMP_MANAGER
FROM    employees emp
        LEFT JOIN employees mgr
        ON emp.emp_supervisor = mgr.emp_id
ORDER BY NVL(mgr.emp_supervisor, 0), emp.emp_last, emp.emp_first;

EMP_FIRST     EMP_LAST        EMP_MANAGER
------------ --------------- --------------
Big           Boss
Rick          Jameson         Big Boss
Adam          Smith           Big Boss
Rob           Stoner          Big Boss
Bill          Abong           Rick Jameson
Janet         Jeckson         Rob Stoner
Fred          Stoneflint      Bill Abong
Alf           Alien           Janet Jeckson
Norm          Storm           Alf Alien
Dell          Aptop           Norm Storm
Top           Gun             Norm Storm
John          Jones           Norm Storm
Noh           Kia             Norm Storm
Phil          McCoy           Norm Storm
John          Picard          Norm Storm
Luke          Skytalker       Norm Storm
James         Thomas          Norm Storm
```

A self join like the above example connects a table back to itself a single time. There is a SQL clause called CONNECT BY PRIOR that performs an operation that acts much like multiple self-joins. One of the more common examples of this function is the ability to create organization charts. With the CONNECT BY PRIOR functionality, it is possible to return results that show the chain of an employee to his manager, to his manager's manager, and so forth. The CONNECT BY PRIOR clause is not actually a join operation and is unlikely to appear on the exam. It is included here to provide a comparison to the way in which a SELF JOIN operation works. It also shows how the recursive relationship in the EMPLOYEES table can be used to generate results in a hierarchical format.

```
SELECT level, emp_first, emp_last, emp_job, emp_id, emp_supervisor
FROM   employees emp
START WITH emp_supervisor IS NULL
CONNECT BY PRIOR emp_id = emp_supervisor;

LEVEL EMP_FIRST  EMP_LAST   EMP_JOB    EMP_ID EMP_SUPERVISOR
----- ---------- ---------- ---------- ------ --------------
    1 Big        Boss       CEO             1
    2 Adam       Smith      CFO             2              1
    2 Rick       Jameson    SVP             3              1
    3 Bill       Abong      VP              5              3
    4 Fred       Stoneflint SrDir           7              5
    2 Rob        Stoner     SVP             4              1
    3 Janet      Jeckson    VP              6              4
    4 Alf        Alien      SrDir           8              6
    5 Norm       Storm      Mgr             9              8
    6 John       Jones      Pilot          10              9
    6 Top        Gun        Pilot          11              9
    6 Phil       McCoy      Pilot          12              9
    6 James      Thomas     Pilot          13              9
    6 John       Picard     Pilot          14              9
    6 Luke       Skytalker  Pilot          15              9
    6 Dell       Aptop      Pilot          16              9
    6 Noh        Kia        Pilot          17              9
    5 Guy        Newberry   Mgr            18              8
```

Domain 6: Transactions, Currency Control and Database Security

6.1 Create transactions and enable currency control

Transactions

A transaction is a logical unit of work in a relational database. When a given operation is part of a transaction, all of the operation should be completed or none of – but never only a portion of it. An example would be an operation that moved money from your savings account to your checking account. One piece of the operation subtracts money from your savings account and the second piece adds that same amount to your checking account. If the operation were to fail after subtracting the money from savings but before adding it to checking, the money would be lost. One way to prevent this in a database is to specifically group multiple individual operations into a transaction.

A database that is guaranteed to process transactions reliably is called ACID-compliant. ACID is an acronym for (Atomicity, Consistency, Isolation, Durability). A database that has transactions that provide these four properties guarantees that transactions will be processed reliably. The definitions of each are:

- **Atomicity** -- This requires that each transaction be "all or nothing". If one part of the transaction fails, the entire transaction fails, and the database state is left unchanged. A compliant system must guarantee atomicity in every situation, including power failures, errors, and crashes.
- **Consistency** -- This property ensures that any given transaction will go from one valid state to another. All changes made by the transaction must be valid according to all constraints, rules, triggers, etc. This does not guarantee the data is correct (i.e. an update is still consistent if it changes someone's name to 'Freed' when it should have been 'Fred'). It simply means the transaction cannot result in the violation of any defined database rules.

- **Isolation** -- This ensures that the concurrent execution of statements in the transaction result in a system state that would be obtained if they were executed serially. Transaction isolation is the primary goal of concurrency control.
- **Durability** -- Once a transaction has been committed, all changes are permanent regardless of power loss, crashes, or errors.

Before beginning, I will note that transactions are another area that is not necessarily handled identically among the RDBMS products from different vendors. The behavior presented here is true for Oracle. The behavior in other relational databases may vary somewhat. A transaction can be started either explicitly or implicitly. One example of the differences between RDBMS vendors is that in Microsoft SQL Server the statement BEGIN TRANSACTION is used to explicitly start a transaction. However, Oracle does not support starting a transaction explicitly. Instead, a transaction is started in a session any time a DML statement is executed in a session if there is not already a transaction started.

A transaction in Oracle is composed of one or more DML statements punctuated by either a COMMIT or a ROLLBACK command. Transactions are a major part of the mechanism for ensuring the database maintains data integrity. The transaction control statements commonly available in relational databases are.

- **COMMIT** – Used to end the current transaction and make permanent all changes performed in it.
- **ROLLBACK** -- Used to undo work done in the current transaction or to manually undo the work done by an in-doubt distributed transaction.
- **SAVEPOINT** -- Used to create a name for a specific system change number (SCN), which can be rolled back to at a later date.

A transaction begins when an initial DML statement is issued against the database. This can be followed by any number of additional DML statements. The transaction will continue until some event causes a COMMIT or a ROLLBACK occurs. Most commonly, this is a statement in the session that specifically executes one of these commands. However other events can force a transaction to end, such as existing a development tool that has pending transactions, shutting down the database, or executing DDL commands (which forces an implicit COMMIT).

Savepoints

When performing DML operations, if transaction control is left to only the COMMIT and ROLLBACK commands, the only options to complete a transaction are to accept everything that has been changed and make the changes permanent or accept nothing and undo everything since the last COMMIT. The SAVEPOINT transaction control statement of Oracle allows there to be a middle ground between the two. With savepoints, you can identify specific locations within the transaction that you can go back to – undoing any DML statements later than that point, but leaving intact all the ones prior to it. The example below shows an example of savepoints.

```
COMMIT;
INSERT INTO employees (emp_id, afl_id, emp_first, emp_last,
                       emp_job, emp_supervisor)
VALUES (30, NULL, 'Adam', 'Apple', 'Pilot', 9);

INSERT INTO employees (emp_id, afl_id, emp_first, emp_last,
                       emp_job, emp_supervisor)
VALUES (31, NULL, 'Bob', 'Hopeful', 'Pilot', 9);

SAVEPOINT A;

INSERT INTO employees (emp_id, afl_id, emp_first, emp_last,
                       emp_job, emp_supervisor)
VALUES (32, NULL, 'Charlie', 'Chafing', 'Pilot', 9);

INSERT INTO employees (emp_id, afl_id, emp_first, emp_last,
                       emp_job, emp_supervisor)
VALUES (33, NULL, 'Dude', 'Whersmicar', 'Pilot', 9);

SAVEPOINT B;

INSERT INTO employees (emp_id, afl_id, emp_first, emp_last,
                       emp_job, emp_supervisor)
VALUES (33, NULL, 'Ed', 'Horse', 'Pilot', 9);
```

There are three places that this transaction can be rolled back to.

- **ROLLBACK TO SAVEPOINT B** – Will undo only the last INSERT statement.
- **ROLLBACK TO SAVEPOINT A** – Will undo the last three INSERT statements.
- **ROLLBACK** – Will undo all five INSERT statements.

Uncommited Transactions

Uncommitted transactions in Oracle are in limbo – it's not certain whether they will ever be permanent and so there is limited access to them. Because they might be reversed, the data required to do so must be retained in the rollback segment indefinitely until the changes are either committed or rolled back. Pending transactions have the following four characteristics:

- The changed data is visible to the user that issued the DML.
- The changed data is NOT visible to any other user.
- The rows with the changed data are locked and cannot be altered by any other user.
- The data prior to the DML can be recovered by rolling back the transaction.

Committed Transactions

Committed transactions in Oracle have been made permanent (although obviously they can be changed with another DML operation). Since they have been made permanent, the portion of the rollback segment holding the prior data is released, and the changed rows made accessible. Committed transactions have the following four characteristics:

- The changed data is visible to all database users.
- The locks on the rows affected by the DML are released and they can be updated.
- The changed data has been made permanent and cannot be reversed with a ROLLBACK.

- Any SAVEPOINTs from the transaction are deleted.

If a DML statement fails due to an error, a constraint violation or some other cause, Oracle will roll the statement back. If there are earlier uncommitted DML operations that succeeded without error, they will not be affected by the rollback of the failed statement. If the failed statement is reason to reverse the earlier DML statements, you can issue an explicit rollback. If the statement can be repaired, then you can fix the failed statement and continue on with the remaining portion of the transaction without having to re-issue the preceding DML operations.

Concurrency control

One requirement of a multi-user relational database is that it handle concurrency. Concurrency in this context is the simultaneous access of the same data by more than one user (both reads and writes). There are four levels of transaction isolation defined by the ANSI SQL standard. The isolation levels are defined in terms of phenomena that must be prevented between concurrently executing transactions.

- **Dirty reads** -- A transaction reads data that has been written by another transaction that has not been committed yet.
- **Nonrepeatable (fuzzy) reads** -- A transaction rereads data it read earlier and determines that another committed transaction has modified or deleted the data.
- **Phantom reads** -- A transaction reruns a query returning a set of rows and finds that another committed transaction has added additional rows that satisfy the same search condition from an earlier run of the same query. Phantom reads are similar to fuzzy reads except that they refer to new data that satisfy a condition rather than changed data.

The four defined levels of isolation and their effectiveness against the preventable phenomena is displayed in the diagram below. A given RDBMS will generally only support some of the possible isolation levels available. For example, Oracle supports the read committed level by default but the serializable isolation level can also be utilized.

Preventable Read Phenomena by Isolation Level

Isolation Level	Dirty Read	Nonrepeatable Read	Phantom Read
Read uncommitted	Possible	Possible	Possible
Read committed	Not possible	Possible	Possible
Repeatable read	Not possible	Not possible	Possible
Serializable	Not possible	Not possible	Not possible

Serializable transactions are generally considered to be the most restrictive level of transaction isolation possible. However, it provides the highest degree of isolation. A serializable transaction operates in an environment that makes it appear as if there are no other users in the database modifying data. Effectively from the state of the user session performing the transaction, the database will be "frozen" at the point in time a query began. The transaction will see the database consistently, at a single point in time. Any changes made by other transactions will not be not visible to it, regardless of how long it takes to execute. Serializable transactions reduce concurrency and are norally only used when this level of isolation is a requirement.

Locks

An RDBMS cannot allow two different people to change the exact same information simultaneously. If this were allowed data integrity would be compromised. If multiple users attempt to update the same record, one way of handling the concurrent access is to grant the first user making the request access to the data and make the second user wait. That said, another significant goal of an RDBMS is to minimize user wait time to the point where it is negligible. The locking behavior of a database should be designed to minimize the times when a wait occurs due to concurrent data access.

The most common method of handling 'waits' as described above is though locks. A lock is defined as a mechanism that prevents destructive interaction between transactions accessing a shared resource. They work to ensure data integrity while allowing maximum concurrent access to data.

Locking behavior is yet another of the factors that varies widely from one RDBMS to another. Any mechanism that tracks locks for an RDBMS uses resources. If the technique used to store locks is wasteful of resources and a sufficiently large number of locks is requested, it can conceivably cause performance issues with the database. Locks come at three basic levels:

- **Row Lock** -- This mechanism locks a single row in the database.
- **Page Lock** -- Some database load rows from disk into memory in what are called pages. The size of a page is not universal, but 8k is a fairly common size. An 8k 'page' might contain dozens, hundreds, or thousands of rows depending on how much space each row takes up. Page locks are acquired against the entire page -- even though not all rows in the page are affected.
- **Table Lock** -- This mechanism locks an entire table of the database.

The least restrictive of the above lock types is obviously the row lock.Thist will only cause another user to wait if they attempt to update the exact same row before the lock is released. The next least restrictive is a page lock. A page lock can prevent concurrent access to potentially thousands of rows while an operation is in progress. Finally a table lock is the most restrictive type possible. It can restrict access to an entire table during an operation. This could potentially be millions of rows.

All relational databases attempt to utilize the least restrictive locking method possible. Page locking and Table locking are generally behaviors that occur from a process called lock escalation. Lock escalation is performed when the number of row locks held by a given operation exceeds a certain threshold. For example, if a given operation exceeds five thousand row locks, it might escalate the locking method to use page locks. After escalation, the operation might need to track only two or three page locks rather than locks for the five-thousand individual rows. This frees up resources. Likewise, given a sufficient number of row and page locks, it is possible for the lock method to escalate to a table level following the same train of logic. Lock escalation may increase user waits due to concurrency issues, but it reduces resource usage.

Not all databases utilize lock escalation. Oracle, for example, will never escalate beyond using row locks to manage concurrency. Page locks do not exist in Oracle at all. Oracle does have table locks, but they are used primarily to facilitate DDL operations. For example, while making a change to a table (such as adding a new column), it is not legitimate for anyone to be performing DML operations against the table. A table lock will be used to prevent DML access while the DDL operation is in progress.

Beyond the three levels of locks mentioned above, databases have a various different subtypes of locks. These are not standardized across RDBMS vendors, so they will not be discussed here. The lock types are designed to ensure that a given lock is only as restrictive as necessary to prevent data inconsistencies from occurring. For example, any DMP against a table in Oracle will generate a lightweight table lock against it. This particular table lock does not prevent other users from updating rows in the table. It simply prevents a full table lock, such as is required for a DDL operation against the table, from being acquired. This is because it is not valid for the table structure to be changed while someone is currently updating data in the table..

Locking behavior is generally left up to the database to perform automatically. There is generally a capability for users to manually invoke locks. However, these are almost invariably more restrictive than what would have been chosen automatically by the database. From a performance standpoint, it is generally best to leave the locking to the DBMS.

When determining whether to lock resources being updated by a DML transaction, there are two possible approaches: pessimistic locking and optimistic locking.

- **Pessimistic Locking** -- In the pessimistic model, a resource is locked from the time it is first accessed in a transaction until the time that the transaction has completed. The resource in question is inaccessible to other transactions during that time. Pu another way, when using pessimistic locking, locks are applied in a fail-safe way. Pessimistic locking is more applicable in an environment where conflicting transactions are likely to occur.
- **Optimistic Locking** -- When using the optimistic locking model, a resource is not locked when first accessed by a transaction. Instead, the state of the resource at the time when it was first accessed is saved. Other database transactions are able to concurrently access the resource and there exists the possibility of conflicting changes. When the resource is about to be updated in persistent storage (COMMITTED), the current state of the resource is read from storage and compared to the state that was saved at the beginning of the transaction. If the two states are different, a conflicting update was made, and the transaction will be rolled back. Optimistic locking is more applicable in an environment where conflicting transactions are unlikely to occur.

Deadlocks

One of the worst possible outcomes of locking is a deadlock situation. A deadlock occurs when two or more users are waiting for data locked by each other. In relational database that support lock escalation, this activity can easily trigger a deadlock condition. In situations where only row-level locks occur, it is much rarer -- but still possible. A deadlock would occur in the following sequence of events:

1. User A updates a row containing data for the employee Allen and does NOT commit the transaction.
2. User B updates a row containing data for the employee Bill and does NOT commit the transaction.
3. User A tries to updates the row containing data for the employee Bill. This update will hang waiting on the lock from User B.
4. User B tries to updates the row containing data for the employee Allen. This update will hang waiting on the lock from User A.

Neither of the above transactions can move forward, hence the sessions are deadlocked. On sessions where a deadlock has occurred, the only solution is for one of the users to issue a rollback so that the other can complete their transaction. Oracle automatically detects deadlock sessions and rolls back one of the user sessions.

6.2 Identify elements of database security

Database security

There are a number of basic security standards which a secure database must ensure:

- **Confidentiality** -- Confidentiality of data means that a database allows individuals to access only the data which their job roles entitle them to.
- **Integrity** -- Ensuring data integrity means that data is protected from deletion and corruption, both while it is in the database, and while being transmitted across a network.
- **Availability** -- Information in the database should always be available to authorized users, without delay. Denial-of-service attacks are attempts to block authorized users' ability to access and use the system when needed.

Securing a database occurs at many different levels and from many different threats. A database can be damaged by someone outside the company who deliberately attempts to do so. However, it is also possible for it to be damaged by a valid employee of the organization who executes a command in the database by accident. For that matter, it can be destroyed by a hardware failure that causes a loss of a data file for which there is no backup. Threats come from multiple different sources and for that reason many completely unrelated measures are required to provide protection against them.

There are at least four tiers involved in securing the information stored in a database. The 1D0-541 exam really should only cover the last two options, and of those, primarily the database. The first two are included just to be thorough. The four tiers are:

- The operating system on which the database is running.
- The network used to access the database.
- Any applications which access the database.
- The database itself.

Operating System

If the operating system that the database files are stored on is poorly secured, it can make any database-level precautions meaningless. For example, if it is easy to gain root-level access to the OS, than it becomes simple to damage or destroy the database, or simply steal the database files. The same is true of root level access is tightly held, but access to the filesystem where the database is stored is freely available. It is important to be sure that the OS is secure and that access to the locations containing the database files and executables is tightly restricted.

Network

Information being transmitted through a network is not always secure. Various techniques exist that allow unauthorized people to view information passing across networks. These include network sniffers, man in the middle attacks, and more. This tier offers the smallest opportunity for direct damage to the database, but if the information on it is extremely sensitive, network security should not be ignored.

Applications

Well written applications will provide an extra layer of security on top of the protections built into the database itself. Unfortunately, poorly-written applications can provide a security hole through which it is possible to bypass the protections built into the database. Applications that access a database should always require user authentication. This is especially true given the fact that an ever-increasing percentage of database applications are web-enabled. Applications should be designed to restrict user actions to the bare minimum required to perform their job duties. Likewise any capabilities for creating queries or generating reports should be restricted to users with applicable job roles. The greater the access and powers granted through an application, the more dangerous it becomes if an unauthorized person gains access to it.

Database

Database security covers a number of different areas including user authentication, user authorization, encryption, and database auditing. If the term is defined broadly enough, it can also be assumed to include disaster recovery. Each of these areas will be discussed in turn.

- **User authentication** -- Any multi-user relational database has a list of valid database users. The database will contain some administration accounts by default. Any accounts with admin-level privileges should be given very strong passwords that are closely-held. User-level accounts should be created as needed and a minimum password complexity requirement imposed on the accounts. As the number of accounts increases, so does the chance that one of them will be compromised by an attacker. Therefore only grant database accounts to people who need them.

- **User authorization** -- One a user has been authenticated, their database access is restricted by the privileges that have been granted to them as discussed earlier in the section on DCL. Grants should be made with the intent of providing the least privileges required for users to perform their job roles. This makes user accounts less dangerous if an attacker manages to steal someone's password. However, much more important is the fact that it minimizes damages that legitimate users can do to the database by accident. An attacker may never gain access to your database, but legitimate users will be logged in every single day.
- **Encryption** -- This is the process of transforming data into an unreadable format using an encryption algorithm. Many databases have a mechanism for encrypting data stored in the data files. This is generally designed to prevent an attacker from being able to gain access to a copy of a data file and then be able to access the data from outside the database. Because there tends to be a performance cost for encrypting and decrypting data, this is normally only used when the data is highly sensitive or confidential.
- **Database Auditing** -- This is the act of monitoring and recording user database actions. Auditing specific database activities can assist in deterring users from inappropriate actions. It is also useful for investigating suspicious activity.
- **Disaster Recovery** -- Developing and following a well-planned backup strategy is absolutely critical for any production database. Backups should be taken on a regular basis. Copies of the backups should be stored both on-site for convenience and off-site to prevent a single disaster from destroying an entire database irretrievably.

ABOUT THE AUTHOR

Matthew Morris has worked with relational databases since 1996 when he worked in the RDBMS support team for Oracle Support Services. Employed by Oracle for over eleven years in support and development positions, Matthew was an early adopter of the Oracle Certified Professional program. He was one of the first one hundred Oracle Certified Database Administrators (version 7.3) and was also in the first hundred to become an Oracle Certified Forms Developer. In the years since, he has upgraded his Database Administrator certification for releases 8i, 9i, 10g, 11g, and 12c; become an Advanced PL/SQL Developer Certified Professional; added the Expert certifications for Application Express, Oracle SQL, and Oracle SQL Tuning.

Matthew is an experienced Database Administrator and PL/SQL developer and has been creating Web applications with Oracle Application Express since the early days of its release. He is the author of the Oracle Certification Prep series of certification guides and has published over twenty books in that series to date.

Made in the USA
Monee, IL
04 November 2026

67378096R00115